The Entitled Generation

Other Books by the Author

The Entitled Generation: Helping Teachers Teach and Reach the Minds and Hearts of Generation Z (2017)
Helping Parents Understand the Minds and Hearts of Generation Z (2017)
Common Sense Education: From Common Core to ESSA and Beyond (2016)
The Wrong Direction for Today's Schools: The Impact of Common Core on American Education (2015)
Teacher-Student Relationships: Crossing into the Emotional, Physical, and Sexual Realms (2013)

The Entitled Generation

Helping Teachers Teach and Reach the Minds and Hearts of Generation Z

Ernest J. Zarra III

ROWMAN & LITTLEFIELD
Lanham • Boulder • New York • London

Published by Rowman & Littlefield
A wholly owned subsidiary of The Rowman & Littlefield Publishing Group, Inc.
4501 Forbes Boulevard, Suite 200, Lanham, Maryland 20706
www.rowman.com

Unit A, Whitacre Mews, 26-34 Stannary Street, London SE11 4AB

Copyright © 2017 by Ernest J. Zarra III

All rights reserved. No part of this book may be reproduced in any form or by any electronic or mechanical means, including information storage and retrieval systems, without written permission from the publisher, except by a reviewer who may quote passages in a review.

British Library Cataloguing in Publication Information Available

Library of Congress Cataloging-in-Publication Data Available

ISBN 978-1-4758-3191-7 (cloth : alk. paper)
ISBN 978-1-4758-3192-4 (pbk. : alk. paper)
ISBN 978-1-4758-3193-1 (electronic)

∞ ™ The paper used in this publication meets the minimum requirements of American National Standard for Information Sciences Permanence of Paper for Printed Library Materials, ANSI/NISO Z39.48-1992.

Printed in the United States of America

This book is dedicated to my wife, Suzi . . .
The hardest working and most gifted teacher I know.
You are my hero!

Contents

List of Tables		ix
Preface		xi
1	Students Then and Now	1
2	Are Gen Z Students Smarter Than Their Technology?	21
3	Teaching to Engage Gen Z	41
4	Expectations of Gen Z Students	69
5	Success with Gen Z	93
Notes		113
Index		125
About the Author		131

List of Tables

Table 3.1	Popular Gen Z apps	50
Table 4.1	Comparison of five American generations	78

Preface

After nearly four decades in the trenches as an educator, I thought I had seen pretty much everything there was to see in education. I have taught in both private and public schools, been a vice principal, served for years as a professional development leader for the largest high school district in the nation, had a blast coaching varsity girls' soccer, and even visited schools in several foreign nations on different continents. Yes, I thought I had seen it all, until, that is, Gen Z came around.

Because I go by the name Dr. Z, the name that my students use to refer to me, I thought it was quite interesting someone would name this current generation of students after me. Alas, I miscalculated that. Well, all kidding aside, the current Gen Z has rewritten many of the rules of teaching and learning, caused theorists to rethink their premises and conclusions, and has exploded the fields of neuroscience, psychology, technology, and a few more.

Gen Z is the first generation to be born that has no recollection of a period of time before cell phones. They do not know a time before the Internet or computers. They also have little to no recollection of September 11, 2001— our nation's modern Pearl Harbor.

It is not cliché to say that Gen Z is unique. They truly are unique. Certainly, every generation can claim uniqueness in one way or another. However, Gen Z has moved the needle culturally, educationally, and generationally in several ways. First, they are addicted to their smart devices and this has implications for schools and families. By the time Gen Z graduates high school, they will have played thousands of hours of video games on their handheld devices and on flat screen monitors meant for mini-stadiums.

Second, Gen Z are the "softest" generation to come along. They lead with their emotions and believe they can discover knowledge and truth through these emotions. They make every effort to prove this by their actions on social media sites and online postings with friends, family, and strangers. Third, Gen Z has a deep sense of entitlement that surpasses even the Millennials, which is matched by more than a mere touch of narcissism.

REASONS FOR WRITING THIS BOOK

As a researcher and education theorist, I decided to delve into this generation to learn more about the students who sit and stare at me each morning. I also wanted to help them learn more about themselves. I can honestly say students relax a bit more when they know a teacher understands them. The other book in this series is written for parents. I wrote that book to assist both the parents and Gen Z children in understanding each other a little better.

As a classroom educator, I desire to know the audience that presents itself every day. I want to know what makes Gen Z tick and what makes them ticked. I also desire to understand the ways Gen Z learns now that they have become so dependent on their technology. I enjoy challenges and I want to discover how the most distracted generation of my time can handle learning and assessments. What new strategies and methods work with Gen Z?

I have seen so many changes occur in my nearly forty years in education. I am noticing two reactions from colleagues locally and across the nation. Some like the advent of Gen Z and their technology and others are learning to despise what tech has done to students. I address these concerns and more in this book.

Teachers have asked me what we can do to either jump in and join the distractions or work against the grain. There is a middle ground and it is addressed in the book as well. Teachers want to succeed and Gen Z wants to succeed. It is time to figure out the best ways to go about success for both.

Once Gen Z teachers begin to inhabit the classrooms, education will shift in many ways. For the time being, teachers can rely on the fact that there are answers to the questions posed to them each day. One of several reasons for undertaking this project is to find ways to assist colleagues with their struggles over what to do with a distracted generation, addicted to its devices and unable to concentrate for more than a few seconds on any one thing. Teachers will see themselves in this book, even though it is a book for them, about Gen Z. Believe it or not, some teachers are the parents of my students.

The more that teachers understand where Gen Z is coming from, the less stress they will experience. Their uniqueness has never really been seen in American public education before. Teacher training institutions are also wrestling with just what to do to prepare Gen Z teachers for an education world that runs at such a slow pace for their brains and energy levels.

INSPIRATION FOR THIS BOOK

As I was finishing this book for teachers, the faces of colleagues who have come and gone flashed before me. I am a person who has learned from some of the very best mentors who could ever have graced a person's life. The men and women who looked into my shy eyes and remarked about my bashful countenance all those many years ago put up with so much from my early days in the classroom. But I learned fast and I learned from some of the very best. They saw something in me that I did not see. I will not embarrass them by name. But I have told them again and again how much I love and appreciate them.

Some of these mentors are no longer with us, but their mentoring and legacy live on in my life. In writing this book, I trust some of their impacts in my life will have been communicated through the words on the pages.

May all the teachers who work in the schools in America, as well as those who homeschool, find that they are not alone in their struggles to understand the changes in culture. Gen Z is squarely in the middle of these changes.

Chapter One

Students Then and Now

> This institution will be based on the illimitable freedom of the human mind. For here we are not afraid to follow truth wherever it may lead, nor to tolerate any error so long as reason is left free to combat it.[1]
> —Thomas Jefferson

Chapter 1 includes the following nine major sections: 1) explosive numbers, 2) a time for reflection, 3) teacher training and gender issues, 4) education and previous generations of students, 5) education and expectations of current Gen Z students, 6) major differences between Gen Z and Millennials, 7) Gen Z at college, 8) strengths and weaknesses of Gen Z students, and 9) conclusion.

Teachers from every generation share the common experiences of students' stories. Baby Boomer, Gen X, and Millennial teachers share their uniquely hilarious interactions with students. Occasionally some of these stories are embellished. But educators reserve that prerogative. Even with teacher embellishment, there are those moments when something a student says or does can only be categorized as off-the-charts outlandish. Such stories fall into the category of *teachers cannot make up this stuff*. In this sense, students are no different than their predecessors.

In a very real sense, today's students are quite different in an assortment of ways. The foundation of these differences lies in how students' brains are developing. This process is referred to as *wiring up*. As a result of living in a high-tech information age, labeling a person or a group is more easily accomplished. Gen Z students have a bevy of labels placed on them today. Compared to previous generations, the likelihood that modern technology has somehow caused brain wiring to be different, resulting in developmental issues for Gen Z students, is not such a farfetched notion. Creative labels could be applied at this point. Suffice it to say that students today are wired differently than students of the past.

EXPLOSIVE NUMBERS

On a serious note, today's students are diagnosed with syndromes, physical disabilities, emotional illnesses, biochemical abnormalities, processing challenges, and a host of other dysfunctions. More and more labels appear and more students are diagnosed with learning challenges. One has to question whether medical and mental health professionals are actually diagnosing new maladies or whether these professionals are hasty in drawing conclusions in their diagnoses.

Challenges in the Classroom

Teachers have unique challenges in every generation. In the past, there were issues of second-language learners, uneducated immigrants, and poverty. Cross-generational issues are similar. However, these issues exist today and, in many corners of the nation, are worse in comparison to the last few decades. Assessment scores are slipping annually. Students are disconnecting from the current educational paradigm. So while these challenges and concerns exist for teachers, each is accentuated by large numbers of students and families that also experience them.

The students arriving in classrooms with predetermined labels bring unique challenges for American teachers. Ranging from the autism spectrum to ADHD to bipolar and back again, teachers of Gen Z are faced with the reality of vast differences in students of just a decade or two ago. Their brains lack significant attention spans. Some students have problems learning content, and processing data is increasingly problematic. The numbers of medicated students are mounting. There are increases in every state for alternative education. As a nation, we must ask ourselves the causes of all of these challenges and contemporary circumstances. Compared to the past, today's schools are much more educational triage for medical and social reasons than they are for teaching and learning and the production associated with learning outcomes.

A TIME FOR REFLECTION

Today's students have documented reasons why they cannot assimilate in public school classrooms without modifications and accommodations to learning, work production, and subsequent assessments. Increasingly, the law and medical professions today support such documentation and teachers must comply with the stipulations that carry the weight of privacy protections of federal and state laws. Education has slowed in many instances because of these obstacles. These obstacles are in no way the children's fault. Nevertheless, the obstacles are real and teachers across two or more decades are justified in reflecting back in time to what children were like in previous generations.

As we advance technologically and scientifically as a nation, we discover more about the human brain. The more we discover about the brain, the more we may find the center of many of today's students' learning issues. Culture in America, usually because of political pressure and progressive ideas making their ways into classrooms, has changed education significantly.

Our nation has lost its focus on the prize because we focus on everything. On a grander scale, it is like American education has its own distraction disorder, looking at everything with resulting mediocrity and doing very little well. Along with the possibility of brain wiring differences, students today are experiencing a surge in educational philosophy that encourages students to identify themselves and discover truth according to their feelings. As most teachers understand, the chemical and biological makeup of tangible elements is not open to feelings.

Popular Trends

A popular sociological phenomenon gaining more and more acceptance in public schools and colleges among today's students is the view that gender expression and sexual identity are fluid.[2] However, not all physicians, researchers, and scholars agree with this.[3] Not all parents agree with this. Regardless of the agreement or disagreement, teachers and counselors are often restricted by law or policy from informing parents of anything along these lines. Student privacy laws allow students to live dual lives in many cases. This may change, beginning in Texas,[4] where parents are gaining ground on behalf of information about their children. The new law enacted in January 2017, the Every Student Succeeds Act (ESSA), is placing much more local control of schools into the hands of communities and out of the hands of the bureaucrats in Washington, DC.[5]

As of now, for example, a fourteen-year-old who is struggling with gender confusion/identity may or may not have his or her parents' support yet be fully supported by his or her school.[6] Teachers must wrestle with issues that just a decade ago were not focal points in America's schools. In many classrooms around the nation, public school teachers are wary of using gender-based pronouns in their daily discourse with students. The misuse of politically correct verbiage could lead to a reportable offense in terms of bias.

Gender neutrality is the newest of education social conditioning attempts. Under the guise of fairness, equity, and social justice, millions of students can question their identities and teachers must walk a fine line on how they reference anyone in their classrooms. In order to avoid conflict, boys may now be "referred to as students or purple penguins."[7] These references may last only as long as the term "student" begins to take on some aspect of bias or makes a child feel less of a person.

TEACHER TRAINING AND GENDER ISSUES

In Lincoln, Nebraska, for example, teachers were given handouts from the group Gender Spectrum,[8] which provides "education, training and support to help create a gender sensitive environment for all children and teens."[9] Also, "teachers in Charlotte, North Carolina have been advised to stop calling the children 'boys and girls,' according to a training presentation on transgender issues."[10]

The nation is undergoing both a neutralization of traditional gender recognition and a replacement with a philosophy that recognizes many genders. Gen Z children are right in the middle of this philosophical experiment. This means that even male or female teachers have to be wary of speaking from their identities in public schools because any gender expression that is binary (male and female) is not viewed as inclusive.[11]

Gender Spectrum explains the importance of the role of schools in affecting change in culture with respect to the changes in traditional gender understanding.

> As one of society's most powerful socializing forces, schools play a crucial role in the manner in which young people make meaning of the world around them. Messages received there have a tremendous impact on how they perceive themselves and others as they receive cues from their educational institu-

tions about what is or is not acceptable. Throughout history, this role has had a tremendous impact, both for good as well as for ill, on how differences across race, language, and disability have been perceived. So too for gender. In a period when perceptions of gender are shifting all around us, our schools once again have the opportunity, and the responsibility, to help lead the way to greater acceptance and inclusion for young people of all genders.[12]

Once a physical, mental, or emotional disability has been identified, the identification often carries special protections. Many times being assigned a designation brings with it some form of government funding. Once that occurs, civil rights then require that students with these conditions be treated as equals in public school classrooms. That being said, what is the set of underlying causes of the differences in the brains of Gen Z children today that they are awakening to new genders?

Could technology be a contributing factor toward these differences and its increasing use a factor in today's classrooms, where some of Gen Z's learning issues are more prominent? Are there any continual effects upon the emotional centers of the developing brain that, because of chemical changes from overuse, can cause residual confusion over one's identity during the developmental years? These are certainly not politically correct questions, but they must be asked because there are serious questions that persist in terms of today's use of technology, brain development, and behaviors that were not prevalent in previous generations. Jim Taylor adds to the discussion by asking, "Who or what is defining your self-identity?"[13]

> One of the most powerful ways in which technology is altering self-identity is through the shift from being internally to externally driven. Yes . . . social factors have always had an impact on the formation of self-identity, but they had been, up until recently, partners of sorts with our own internal contributors to self-identity. But now the sheer ubiquity and force of the latest technological advances has taken that influence and turned its volume up to a deafening roar.
>
> In previous generations, most of the social forces that influenced our self-identities were positive; parents, peers, schools, communities, extracurricular activities, even the media sent mostly healthy messages about who we were and how we should perceive ourselves. Yes, there were bad influences, but they were far outweighed by those that were beneficial. These forces acted mostly as a mirror reflecting back on us what we saw in ourselves, resulting in affirmation rather than change in our self-identities.
>
> But now, the pendulum has swung to the other extreme in a social world where the profit motive rules and healthy influences are mostly drowned out

by the cacophony of the latest technology. The self-identities of this generation of young people and, in fact, anyone who is deeply immersed in popular culture and media, are now shaped by external forces.[14]

Taylor makes an excellent point. Self-identities are shaped differently today than in years past. There is more to bombard and tempt the brains of developing minds and hearts for Gen Z to try something new. Are the voices of new identities calling out Gen Z children and young adults or are children calling out their fluid inner voices and verifying them with media and popular personalities?

EDUCATION AND PREVIOUS GENERATIONS OF STUDENTS

The point has already been established that public school Gen Xers and Millennials moved through their schooling with fewer labels placed upon them. Certainly, Baby Boomers had even less. The norms and traditions of schools of even a decade ago were very different.

Certainly, public education and those willing to experiment with new directions for learning and methods of instruction and assessment should be applauded. Changes in both federal and state administrations brought supposedly newer and better programs to public schools over the years. Frankly, the applause dies down very quickly these days. Veteran teachers chortle when new programs are introduced to their districts. There is a popular refrain quick to fall off the lips of veteran teachers; that is, "Just wait a few years and education programs will retool, and once again repeat themselves."

How many recall the New Math of a few decades ago? The program went the way of the New Coke. At least the marketplace listened and was unafraid to return to its classic product. Bureaucrats' mistakes take years to undo, if they listen at all. How many Americans remember Values Clarification, Reading across the Curriculum, 100% Proficiency Rates by 2014, as well as high stakes testing under No Child Left Behind? The jury is still out on Common Core and the Every Student Succeeds Act (ESSA). The former remains unpopular and is on the chopping block with the Trump administration. The latter is still too new to evaluate whether it will be effective toward returning local education control to communities. But this is where public education finds itself today. Gen Z children are the newest cohort to be in the middle of another education experiment.[15]

In the past, classroom seat time meant so much more than it does today. In public school classrooms today, just keeping children in their seats is a massive challenge, especially in the lower grades. Some teachers are told that students have ADHD and must be allowed to walk around the room as they choose. Instruction is supposed to be differentiated so that each child will feel validated in the learning environment, whether standing or sitting. Others with certain dysfunctions are sometimes allowed to shout out and scream because it is part of their accommodation if they have Asperger's syndrome or a tic.

Disobedient students are sometimes labeled as victims from their home life and therefore not truly responsible for lashing out at others during the day. At the junior high and high school levels, students in the past were reprimanded and disciplined for cutting classes. Culture has changed so much that what counts more are schools' average daily attendance (ADA) numbers for funding. Money still talks louder than any unruly group of students.

Old School versus New School

Students in the past were told by parents that they were graduating from high school. Many were also told they were going on to college to complete a degree, then off to earn a living. In fact, this was the primary method to higher earnings for most. The children who experienced this passed on this set of expectations as the family paradigm. Gen Z parents still believe in this method of building success, and so do recent Gen Z college grads. However, there is also a rapidly growing number of students who actually view it a little differently, as will be discussed in this chapter.

Graduation for the "old-school" Gen Xers was a fixed, normed set of classes and credits. Technology ranged from film strips, sixteen-millimeter movies with clicking projectors, as well as overhead projectors, complete with blue-palmed teachers. Chalkboards, the Cold War, and economic booms are part of their history. As with all generations, things change and history is made according to the changes. Whoever it is that is empowered to write the books about past generations gets to shape the content. In this regard, Americanism was preeminent in history texts.

Dependence versus Reliance

There is some overlap of context and technology between Millennials and Gen Z. There is in fact overlap across many generations. However, as is explored in chapter 2, the ways technology and communications are used and their importance in daily lives are actually extremely different between Generations Y and Z. One major difference in technology between different generations alive today is the difference between its use and reliance.

For example, Gen Z maintains the posture that their smartphones and constant connectivity are essentials for daily living, often remaining connected twenty-four hours a day. As students, Gen Zers are probably far too young to remember anything of substance about the nation's modern Pearl Harbor, September 11, 2001. Some use 9/11 as the benchmark event, pinpointing and marking the genesis and emergence of Gen Z.

Among Gen Z there is a specific and heavy reliance on smartphones. This reliance can also be referred to as a dependency. Not a minute goes by in many classrooms in America where students are not sending or receiving messages. There is an emotional awareness to being connected, kind of like being in love with love. By contrast, Millennials are not as entrenched in their use of technology. They are utility-based, for the most part, and not dependent on being connected *all day, every day* by their devices. They still use devices for many things, but Gen Z outpaces them as a generation.

Millennials certainly do not sleep with their phones next to their pillows and do not spend inordinate amounts of time online playing video games, sending and receiving text messages and Snapchats, and watching movies prior to bedtime.[16] Developing brains need down time and sleep to make proper neural connections. Are these connections lacking in the brains of Gen Z, now that teddy bears have been replaced by smartphones by so many students?

Parents of Gen Zers have done their children no real favors by providing them with smartphones. Reasons for this are discussed in chapter 2. As students, Gen Zers are bound to their technology. In fact, they are addicted. They expect others in their lives to acquiesce to their addiction and understand their "need" to be connected. This addiction plays out at schools and even on the sidelines at athletic competitions. Advocates of Gen Z and professionals who study this generation are repeating the exhortation that teachers and schools had better get on board to determine how they plan to meet Gen Z's demand for education "their way."

EDUCATION AND EXPECTATIONS OF CURRENT GEN Z STUDENTS

Schools cannot meet the needs of all children. No one can meet the needs of the whole of each child. It makes a nice slogan and a wonderful school motto. Communities respond to the wonderful rally cry that schools should be *all things to all people*. Yet as a culture the nation is far too focused on which restroom and locker room should be used by a small percentage of Americans.

Such distractions are in the way of education. Of course, these issues are important political issues. Nevertheless, schools should not be about making certain that all children come away with an engineered, alternate view of gender and marriage over and against deepening mathematical reasoning, critical thinking, linguistic proficiency, global and domestic competition, and academic assessments.

Is it any wonder assessment scores are stagnant? Please do not miss the point. If America expects its students and its schools to compete academically, ultimately producing students who will impact our nation's economy, then public education cannot be all things to all people without sacrificing education along the way. There is no slight intended in dealing with facts.

Students today are being engineered to focus on social causes. Gen Z feels its way into truth, considering emotions as factual as two plus two equals four in mathematics. Graduation rates are up for Gen Z. However, where are we in a competitive sense? The literacy rates for students have decreased on state scores, thanks in no small measure to Common Core. The United States continues to fall behind other nations in mathematics. For example, the most recent Programme for International Student Assessment (PISA) assessment, given in 2015, shows that American fifteen-year-olds have dropped precipitously in comparison to seventy-two other nations that were assessed. The 11 percent decline in mathematics scores is "the biggest decrease in the subject for American students since 2009, the last year that the scores improved."[17]

Softies. One of the knocks on Gen Z is that they have been raised to be "soft." That is, the students of Gen Z are easily manipulated by emotions and therefore quite pliable in social conditioning and causes that play to these emotions. Today's students are similar to students of the past in that they are affected by popular culture. That will probably never change. However, Gen Z is dissimilar in its reluctance to hold views that are different from popular culture for fear of admonishment and being somehow disconnected from the popular trends online. Gen Z is a willing participant in moral and social inveigling, brought to them by the elites they tend to worship through Twitter feeds and Snapchat alerts.

Gen Z is soft on tackling life's harshest difficulties, often seeking to be bailed out or to blame someone else for their circumstances. The Gen Zers are also noted for being soft on earning their own way in athletics, academics, college admission, and employment. Teachers must deal with parents who stop by to solve dile mmas for their children. Take for example school districts that are now being blamed for doing too much for students and families that education is taking a backseat. Some argue that schools have taken on so much that a primary reason for schools in the twenty-first century is to focus more on the social programs and caring for students as larger families in context.

Teachers do few favors for Gen Z students when the first thing that is asked of students in this generation is to apply feelings to what they learn in class. Emotions do have their place in the classroom and they serve as excellent motivators to student learning. However, the first question in the classroom should not be, "So, how do you feel about this issue or that set of concerns?" Feelings should not be the drivers of education. This opens too many doors for teachers to manipulate students toward a certain agenda. It also continues to perpetuate Gen Z's reputation as softies.

Instead of leading with feelings and emotions, teachers ought to be asking, "What are your thoughts about this situation, or that situation, and explain the plans you have to reduce, expand, or change these concerns?" Feelings are secondary and tertiary because they change so very quickly and holding feelings or emotions to a constant among students is nearly impossible. Anyone having taught junior high or high school understands this reality. Elementary school is a different emotional creature altogether.

Takers. Gen Z has been raised to be selective *takers.* However, consider that this generation has been taught that their presence at events, the selective association with activities—hence their mere existence—entitles them to awards and various things of equality of outcome. Gen Z generally expects to be provided these things, with any level of effort expended, yet usually at someone else's expense.

Schools today have become major social institutions, mimicking government philosophies and practicing mandates politically. Andrew Rotherham illustrates this point: "School . . . officials are thinking about transporting students to school, what they'll feed them, health services for them, sports teams and schedules, and all the other things we call on school districts to do. Meanwhile, if you're lucky, someone might also be focused on who is going to teach your child and what they're going to teach."[18]

Schools as Families

Some families now insist that school districts should directly support and implement various social programs that have as their goal not only to educate, but to add support in raising children. This amounts to meals, government-subsidized housing, counseling, transportation, "free" programs, and financial offsets. There is nothing wrong with people caring for people, and children are those for whom we most definitely must care. However, are schools meant to be the new primary care facilities? Where have we gone as a society that schools are becoming replacement primary caregivers for children?

Time is a precious element in schools. Efforts to focus on social engineering not only detract from limited educational time, but they also step into a zone meant exclusively for the family. What is the answer? Communities must help to fix the family. Families then must step up and fix themselves. Schools can help engage the community aggressively to support two-parent and single-parent households. Schools must get back to supporting the family and not become content with surrogacy. In the first book of this series, *Helping Parents Understand the Minds and Hearts of Generation Z*, ideas are presented for parents and teachers, local schools, and community organizations to join together in support of local families. It is time we revisit the building blocks of our local communities.

What is left to ponder when lifting academic achievements and literacy rates are the stated primary focus of education, yet as a system it has seen fit to shift to the place once predominantly occupied by the nuclear family? All things considered, is it to anyone's surprise that "lack of focus is one reason instructional quality remains so uneven within schools, districts, and around the country?"[19]

MAJOR DIFFERENCES BETWEEN GEN Z AND MILLENNIALS

Differences between Gen Z and other generations are good to know for teachers. Instructional methods and the learning environment can be adjusted to accommodate the differences in styles of learning. Accommodate they must. Gen Z learns somewhat differently from even its immediate generational predecessor, the Millennials.

Gen Z has a shortened attention span. It believes it is better at multitasking. The young adults of Gen Z care about bargain hunting when shopping for goods and services, are admittedly becoming good planners, and stereotypically begin projects earlier.[20] They use Internet search engines in ways that many shop.

Many Gen Z college graduates are enthralled about exercising their entrepreneurial spirit when it comes to career planning and employment. This makes Gen Z carry the reputation of wanting to work for a living their own way and according to their own terms.[21] However, the generation still respects the traditional college route to success as an idea. Society must question whether this respect will be maintained much longer.

Such thinking with regard to work has enabled researchers to define Gen Z as a group that seems to have higher expectations than previous generations. Unfortunately, not all of Gen Z's expectations are grounded in reality, which is an aspect of youthfulness combined with hefty daily doses of Internet propaganda. The consolation is that they can change expectations as quickly as they set them in the first place. So stability of lifestyle may be called into question.

One other generational distinction classifying Gen Z as unique is that it is individually focused as well as globally focused. Performing well on the global stage economically equates to performing well individually,[22] according to those who have already graduated college. How these global aspects take shape with Gen Z is less clear.

Feelings Are Not Enough

One might ask, how in the world can high school graduation rates be over 80 percent nationally, yet the graduates are scarcely literate? That is an excellent question. The answer lies in the softness of the generation, perpetuated by the entitled mentality. Focusing on emotions through programs such as social justice, coupled by political correctness and accepting funding from the government, has shifted students away from learning. Rather than empowering academics and reasoning before taking action, students are supposed to feel responsive. This is partly where our system has gone off the rails. Focus on issues that are best left to homes takes away from the learning environment to which parents entrust their children.[23] Students cannot feel their way to success in science and math and they certainly cannot be allowed to feel their way to diplomas.

The Kindnesses of Hearts

A recent example in California illustrates the larger point to be made. California tossed out its high school graduation exit exam requirement (CAHSEE) and as a result went back to the turn of the twenty-first century and retroactively granted diplomas to students who were not eligible to graduate at that time. California is not alone in this change of educational philosophy. Apparently, it was not socially just or fair that students who did not pass one or more sections of the exam would be kept from earning the same thing as students who actually passed the exam.

Feeling that some students were harmed by the test led students to be labeled as casualties of that test. Kind-hearted bureaucrats determined that certain students in the past should not be without diplomas, so let's blame the test and give them all a certificate of completion. This is where political correctness and votes overlap with educational philosophy.

In the final analysis, students are now becoming casualties of the feelings of those with a social agenda. Kind people seek to subvert any capitalist notion that earning something has merit and that the real world is a harsh and competitive place. If schools continue to demonstrate that they are no longer places where everyone must earn their way, then high school diplomas will take on less meaning as a result.

In the case of California, being given a high school diploma without completely earning it "feels" to critics like it is an equivalent to a participation certificate. Giving away diplomas for attendance or because someone feels it was wrong to withhold diplomas because of an assessment failure is an example of social justice gone awry. Everyone getting a diploma by going through the system lessens the value of the diploma and does little to encourage already unmotivated groups of students to do little more than show up to socialize. Again, how does this bolster education and provide more competitive students? America should cease experimenting with students.

Not Good Enough?

Another example of the softness of Gen Z is found in Tallahassee, Florida. "A girl not chosen to be a high school cheerleader . . . threatened legal action against the school district if . . . not put on the team."[24] "Despite threats that some cheerleaders would quit the team if the usual selection process of earning one's place on the team was not followed, the school district . . . overruled cheerleading judges in the past, intervening when certain girls did not make the teams" at other schools in the area.[25] This is a Gen Z phenomenon and is becoming more commonplace each year. Please remember that Gen Z students have Gen Z parents, meaning that some parents of Gen Z students hold certain entitlement expectations and demonstrate these expectations through surprising behaviors. The implication of this declaration is quite clear.

There is social status for males and females to be on teams and often athletes may think more highly of themselves than reality portrays. That comes with on-field success. Looking good in the uniform lasts only as long as the pregame warmup. There is more than image involved. No one wants to be sued when feelings are hurt. Students in the past were cut from squads and they had to learn to deal with the reality that their efforts might not have been good enough. However, to parents of Gen Z children, this is not good enough. In the words of one parent referencing a similar situation, "Your word no is a starting point for my word yes."

A Point in Common

Gen Z also has something else in common with Millennials. There is this joint notion that everyone gets a trophy and that everything should be fair to them as individuals, even if it is not fair to others' efforts.[26] The generation feels entitled because they showed up.[27] A quick anecdote illustrates this point.

Colleagues have often complained that failing students believe they deserve to pass because they come to school and turn in some work. The quality of the work is not significant. Unfortunately, some colleagues bend and give in, using emotions to qualify grading procedures. The closer Gen Z gets to occupying the majority of public school classrooms, the greater the distance between education across the generations.

Gen Z is indeed the entitlement generation, taking what the Millennials believed and fortifying it with expectations and practice. This sense of "I deserve it" did not originate with Gen Z. Parents of any generation who did not think their child had been given something he or she deserved brought quick attention to the person they believed could rectify the situation. The difference today is that threats are made to those at the highest levels of authority, and parents usually get their way. In the case of the cheerleader's tryout, the girl fell twice, giving her an inadequate lower score. She and her parent felt her falls should not be held against her making the team.[28] Doesn't everyone just deserve to be a cheerleader, anyway?

GEN Z AT COLLEGE

Gen Z passed a milestone with its first college graduating class of 2016. Gen Z is establishing the new college and university atmospheres on campuses. What is happening on college campuses in America today is again detracting from education. Safe spaces and safe zones are created for students to avoid hearing anything that might offend them.

Rather than college being the place of expansion of one's thinking, it is becoming, for some, a place to hide and protect themselves from disagreement. Essentially, colleges today are acting as parents in bailing out the students who might have an issue with a person or a group. The extreme emotional reactions to dissent are often the result of another college student's emotions or difference of opinion. Those colleges that offer havens from some of the pressures of the world also have advocates in professors. Young people attending many colleges are experiencing a radical extension of what they learned at home or at secondary school. The softness of today's Gen Z at college is probably as squishy as it gets.

Hey, It Worked in Class!

Recently, a Gen Z student who had a somewhat easy time getting his way at college by making complaints made a fuss at the place of his business internship. The college student brought his college complaint approach into his internship in the real world of business. This young man was aghast at what happened and recently sent correspondence to an advice columnist.

The intern expressed his desire for the company to move to a dress code more to his liking. So in typical Gen Z collegial fashion, he drew in others his age and spoke with them about his concern. His fellow interns agreed to support a proposal for a newer and more lax dress code. Because some interns noticed that one older female worker was allowed to violate the dress code with improper footwear, they thought it was only fair for them to change the dress code to favor themselves. They even drafted a petition for the company to sign and sent it to the administrative management of the company. The following excerpt is how Gen Z met the real world.

The next day, all of us who signed the petition were called into a meeting where we thought our proposal would be discussed. Instead, we were informed that due to our "unprofessional" behavior, we were being let go from our internships. We were told to hand in our ID badges and to gather our things and leave the property ASAP.

We were shocked. The proposal was written professionally like examples I have learned about in school, and our arguments were thought out and well-reasoned. We weren't even given a chance to discuss it. The worst part is that just before the meeting ended, one of the managers told us that the worker who was allowed to disobey the dress code was a former soldier who lost her leg and was therefore given permission to wear whatever kind of shoes she could walk in. You can't even tell, and if we had known about this we would have factored it into our argument.[29]

Institutions of higher learning are supposed to prepare students for the real world and to be ready to step in and work side by side with other generations. Instead, many colleges are catering to the same mindset that followed Gen Z throughout school. That might work while they are students with coddling teachers. The unfortunate thing is that colleges feel they need to succumb to the selfish student notions that whatever some students want, they should get. The real folly is that when some professors do not give in, these professors may be disciplined and even investigated. Others may be reprimanded for encouraging open debate in class.[30]

Higher education is slipping in its preparation of students for the real world. Did anyone stop to tell the brazen young interns that taking such a risk as a young adult could damage their career options? The reality is easy to recognize. Many colleges are doing a huge disservice to students by "treating every petition or pet cause as valid"[31] and celebrating these actions as part of an overall acceptance of behaviors, often applauded by some of the faculty.

SENSITIVITIES OF GEN Z STUDENTS

In schools across America, including postsecondary institutions, there are some strange goings-on. Groups are emerging each day attempting to "scrub campuses clean of words, ideas, and subjects that might cause discomfort or give offense."[32] Some musicians, comedians, politicians, authors, and guest speakers have either declined invitations, backed out of scheduled appearances, or been booed off stage at colleges and universities.

Comedians "Jerry Seinfeld and Bill Maher have publicly condemned the oversensitivity of college students, saying many of them can't take a joke."[33] Gen Z graduates are moving out into the workplace, including taking their places at the fronts of classrooms as teachers. They bring with them their training, temperaments, and tactics for teaching. It remains to be seen whether what students learned will translate to success in the teaching profession.

Campus scrubbing of anyone or anything offensive has brought along with it a few newer concepts of more recent origin. In fact, the application of these concepts exploded in popularity under the Obama administration. The Departments of Justice and Education "greatly broadened the definition of sexual harassment to include verbal conduct that is simply 'unwelcome'" in 2013.[34] As a result of these changes, the old 2003 standard of identifying and defining harassment by means of the "reasonable person test,"[35] which had to go beyond "the mere expression of views, words, symbols or thoughts that some person finds offensive,"[36] was liberalized to basically anything deemed untoward and emotionally unwelcome. Essentially, a great number of Gen Zers are soft and easily hurt by what appears to be political correctness run amok.[37] The real world outside college should provide wakeup calls for the next generation of teachers.

The implications for teachers are enormous. Policies like those of the previous administration make it difficult to teach history, literature, or even art. Teachers are being indoctrinated to provide "trigger warnings" about what students are about to encounter. To be fair, our society has gone the route of putting warning labels on everything from food to cable programs to movies and video games. Essentially, a trigger warning from a professor or teacher is a warning that someone might find the forthcoming offensive. This seems fair, but is it really necessary?

One of the characteristics of Gen Z is their desire to call or contact an authority over something that upsets them[38] or take their gripes to social media, where viral videos cause ruination at the speed of light.[39] The fear is that this new form of protectiveness "may be teaching students to think pathologically."[40] Therein lies the concern about trigger warnings, especially if the warning is incomplete or inaccurate in reference to students' feelings.

This form of protectiveness has many asking, "What are the effects of this new protectiveness on the students themselves? Does it benefit the people it is supposed to help? What exactly are students learning when they spend four years or more in a community that polices unintentional slights, places warning labels on works of classic literature, and in many other ways conveys the sense that words can be forms of violence that require strict control by campus authorities, who are expected to act as both protectors and prosecutors?"[41]

Some Gen Z students today practice a peculiar form of emotional reasoning as a mechanism to determine reality. Emotional reasoning, according to David Burns, is the practice of allowing negative emotions to dictate the way things really are. As a result, if a person feels something, it follows that those feelings are truly what comprises reality. Therefore, based on emotions, what is true for one is not true for another.

Philosophical Perspectives

In Gen Z there is a modified reprise of the subjective and irrational philosophies that made their way around during the 1970s. At that time, students were espousing an "If it feels good, do it" and a "Do what you want, as long as it does not hurt anyone but yourself" set of beliefs. Frankly, the concept of motivated reasoning is the spontaneous generation of "arguments for conclusions"[42] that people already want to support. In some sense, it is a form of emotional deduction, and the facts are created by emotions and not the other way around. Burns elaborates regarding two principles of emotional reasoning.

> Your emotional reaction is generated not by the sentences you are reading but by the way you are thinking. The moment you have a certain thought and believe it, you will experience an immediate emotional response. Your thought actually creates the emotion. The second principle is that when you are feeling depressed, your thoughts are dominated by pervasive negativity. You perceive not only yourself but the entire world in dark, gloomy terms. What is even worse—you'll come to believe things really are as bad as you imagine them to be. If you are substantially depressed, you will even begin to believe that things always have been and always will be negative.[43]

Robert Leahy and Stephen Holland, two cognitive therapists, and Lata McGinn, a psychologist, contend that once feelings guide a person's interpretation of reality, this can lead to one or more cognitive disorders. This is especially the case with depression and bipolar disorder.[44] The truth is, "If everyone around you acts as though something is dangerous—elevators, certain neighborhoods, novels depicting racism—then you are at risk of acquiring that fear too."[45] This appears to be what is happening among Gen Z and one cannot help but question the origin.

The slogan of the 1970s, "If it feels good, it must be good," is now "If I feel it, it must be real." Emotional reasoning is embraced by Gen Z and, as Jonathan Haidt purports, "Emotional reasoning dominates many campus debates and discussions. A claim that someone's words are 'offensive' is not just an expression of one's own subjective feeling of being offended. It is, rather, a public charge that the speaker has done something objectively wrong. It is a demand that the speaker apologize or be punished by some authority for committing an offense."[46] This reality has prompted many college professors and free speech advocates to wonder, "What are we doing to our students if we encourage them to develop extra thin skin just before they leave the cocoon of adult protection?"[47] Veteran teachers may soon be colleagues with these college graduates.

Political Implications

Today, those on the political margins understand that to engage students they must use their emotions. Emotions get people to act. There is great distress in thinking that emotions are weaponized for the sake of scoring political points or to achieve an agenda for one group or another. The interesting thing about emotional reasoning is that it does not have to follow a logical path for emotions to create reality. Emotions are predicated on feelings of the person in question.

Teachers should avoid using student emotions as ploys to accomplish an underlying agenda. They should never allow emotions to be used against those of dissenting viewpoints or competing ideologies. Emotions as truth, when used to belittle, badger, and injure one's opponent, are more hurtful in the long run than any verbal dissent based on philosophical arguments.

Schools and universities have the obligation to prepare students to meet the challenges of the world in which they will participate throughout adulthood. May it never be mentioned among our colleagues that teachers and professors "may be training students in thinking styles that will damage their careers and friendships, along with their mental health."[48]

CONCLUSION

Students from previous generations did not have to wrestle with many of the issues facing today's Gen Z students. Schools were places of education and socialization. Today, schools have become parental surrogates and social institutions, along with their education mandates. Students over the years have had to endure educational experimentation with one program or another, for one reason or another. These experimentations usually came with a context, such as the Cold War, Space Race, or medical advancements.

Gen Z parents have stepped in to assist their children and the children have developed expectations of entitlement. Schools and colleges have acquiesced to these expectations in creating safe spaces or disallowing competing ideas on campuses. Such practices are setting up Gen Z for a fall once they enter the marketplace seeking employment that fits their desires.

Emotional reasoning is taking Gen Z by storm. Political forces have combined with social causes to promote particular social agendas. Teachers being trained for the classroom will soon bring their emotional reasoning into the classroom and apply it to their academics. Teachers of previous generations who are still employed will have to reckon with the way Gen Z views the world.

In closing, it is the job of every teacher to challenge students to think and to realize that he or she must earn his or her place in society. Expecting everything to be handed to them with minimal effort or because they are somehow special as people is not practical in the real world. Gen Z has many wonderful attributes. It is up to all teachers of this nation to tap into these attributes for the sake of the future of the United States.

Chapter Two

Are Gen Z Students Smarter Than Their Technology?

Chapter 2 includes the following six major sections: 1) an inch deep and a mile wide, 2) successful Gen Z students, 3) Gen Z and digital literacy, 4) is Gen Z ready for college? 5) smart technology and the trust factor, and 6) conclusion.

AN INCH DEEP AND A MILE WIDE

The obvious answer to the question asked in the title of this chapter is that Gen Z certainly thinks so! But what does it mean to be smarter than one's technology? Could it mean that those using a certain device are proficient in the use of icons, posts on social media, and performance of Internet searches? Is the answer found in knowledge of the latest online fads and the ability to use several applications on the same cell phone? Frankly, Baby Boomers and even the older traditional generations have smartphones and find them user-friendly. Some colleagues have fatter thumbs than others, but that is another issue.

Smart technology users are familiar with downloading apps from the iTunes or Google Play stores. Some techies have even designed and sold their own apps. Nevertheless, downloading is made easy for the masses. This includes music, whether playing it on Pandora or paying a fee for access. By virtue of all of this, one would have to argue that user-friendliness has removed a prerequisite of deeper intelligence in order to use smart technology.

The way things are today, the playing field has been leveled by the smartness of the technology and not the intelligence of the user.

Chances are there are some members of Gen Z who are much smarter than those who program and design smartphones. Certainly, the chances are great that the devices held in the hands of millions each day surpass the "smartness" of their handlers. What then does this imply for Gen Z students and their devices? The reality is that Gen Z students may not be smarter than their technology and devices, but they can certainly be much smarter by using it. Now this is a difference worth noting for all generations.

A Wider or Deeper Gen Z?

Even with all of their access to technology, its tools and applications that are designed for students to excel, the reliance on smart technology does lead to some serious questions. These questions have much to do with preparing Gen Z students for their futures. One overarching concern translates primarily into matters of preparation and qualification for graduation from high school. A second concern is whether Gen Z is wider in knowledge than they are in depth of understanding. Consequently, as teachers there is a question as to whether Gen Z's advanced proficiency with technology is readying all students for success in higher education and beyond.[1]

Everyone Meant for College?

The data from colleges and universities are not encouraging. The reality is that more and more college students are having to remediate in English-language arts and mathematics during their first years at college. International assessment scores are down. SAT and ACT averages show very little change year to year, and college entrance placement assessment scores rank students in remedial classes about one-third of the time. How is this even possible when the nation is told students' grades are good enough to graduate high school and even good enough to be near the tops of their classes? It is occurring because of the emphasis on graduation over academics and because grade point averages are more difficult to norm than standardized assessments. High school graduation data look quite suspect.

Assessments Optional?

Either college is too hard, high schools are too easy, or both are true. Yet these are not the sole issues facing Gen Z today. Another issue that directly affects today's students is the SAT and ACT exams. The new trend today is to make them optional or do away with the exams completely as measures for incoming college freshmen. An incentive like this is very different from what the Millennials, Gen Xers, and Baby Boomers had to face if they chose to attend college. The rigors of entrance were much more substantive and competitive for previous generations. Keep in mind the question asked at the beginning of this chapter.

In addition, students today admitted to junior or community colleges are not required to take any national admissions assessments. Often they take institution-based exams for placement, but not for admission. Issues such as ease of entrance into community colleges place very little pressure on incoming first-year students to leave high school with any sort of rigorous academic schedule. There is also the reality that not all students are motivated to attend college directly out of high school and that some are truly not meant for college. There is great difficulty in garnering support for this conclusion because politicians and bureaucrats rhetorically press for all students to attend college.[2]

If Americans heeded the challenges laid out for them by Barack Obama, they would come to the conclusion that everyone should go to college and that it should not cost them anything. Teachers know that if there is no skin in the game for students, appreciation levels decline. In fact, it is actually human nature that if something is not earned, a sense of entitlement develops. The failings of Common Core pointed out that American students are clearly either unready for college or university or not able to tackle such a challenge.

How can anyone forget the Bush-era No Child Left Behind (NCLB) legislation that targeted 100 percent of all students in American public schools toward proficiency in math and reading by 2014? The argument is that students are more proficient in technology and learn very differently today than even the previous generation. While this may be true, why are students lacking high school grade-level proficiency and allowed to graduate, ready for college and career, while lacking proficiency for college success? One of the answers may be in the reduction of academic rigor in American schools.

Reducing the Rigor

The removal of a college requirement for admission only validates critics' complaints that rigor and challenge have diminished over the years. There is the appearance that student intelligence is going in the opposite direction of technology. That being said, institutions of higher education still expect graduating high school students to already possess certain skills when they arrive at college. What happens from elementary school to the time students graduate high school?

Either there is something drastically wrong with the students' abilities in general or the system in which they are moving is woefully weak. Is it both? Is it possible that all of America's teachers are somehow doing a poor job? One major contributing factor to the weakness of American students is the use of technology for social reasons and for less academic uses.

Removing college requirements so that all who would apply would have a much greater chance of entrance does not make it seem like college admission is as competitive as it was in previous generations. Rather than keeping admission standards high, colleges are responding to what now seems to have brought public school mediocrity from a place on the horizon into focus in the foreground. Evidence of this mediocrity is in nearly three hundred colleges and universities in America that now have testing for admission to their institutions as purely optional.[3] Are we now at the point where college entrance and diplomas are going to carry similar value as a certificate of participation?

Removing the SAT, the ACT, or other assessments to gain entrance into college is merely a way to accommodate a generation of students that might otherwise not qualify for college admission. This admission does not violate some politically correct principle. Admitting this, however, means the nation has to consider the alternatives for students after high school.[4]

Students are smarter with technology but seem to have lost something in the process. They have lost the rigor required for critical thinking. The processors built into smart technology seem to be outsmarting and outdistancing the abilities of users to process for themselves. How does all of this shake out for the future of Gen Z?

What Does It Mean?

Elementary through junior high are special developmental years for students. There is a natural love of learning and an acceptance of others as friends and collaborative work partners. The growth of intelligence in those years and in those grades provides evidence of several factors contributing to this growth. These include wonderful teachers sacrificing for their students, as well as dedicated and loving families that spend time working with their children. Nevertheless, something happens during the teenage years. Friends begin to mean more than teachers and parents. Gen Z is more device-social and academics are incorporated into this reality.

In some high schools, homework has also become a thing of the past. Rather than spend time completing assignments, students spend several hours a day online posting videos and photos, playing games, listening to music, and sending messages. Being a smart high school or college student means so much more than using a smart device or figuring out how to win a game on a handheld controller. Being smart is also much more than filling in bubbles on a multiple choice assessment.

Smartness brings with it certain character traits and behaviors that incorporate knowledge. Smartness applies who the person is to what the person does, relating these to circumstances and critically thinking about solutions, thereby creating new knowledge. Certainly, smartness is more than knowing how to do something or knowing where to find some knowledge on a topic. Smartness is also the ability to take this knowledge, analyze benefits and costs, and understand consequences, both those intended and unintended, in terms of actions and inactions.

SUCCESSFUL GEN Z STUDENTS

Researchers and "education experts think that character traits such as grit, perseverance and conscientiousness play a role"[5] in determining success at college. In fact, the University of Pittsburgh and the University of Toronto joined forces on a study that focused on teenage Gen Z students. The students were described as "thrivers and divers." The results of the study, performed by researchers Graham Beattie, Jean-William Laliberte, and Philip Oreopoulos, gave students personality quizzes "to determine which traits correlated with college success."[6]

The researchers discovered that those labeled "thrivers" performed better in college, were better adjusted, and earned higher scores in college classes. Thrivers' high school scores were excellent predictors of their potential college success. Those labeled "divers" did much worse. Coming out of high school, the divers lacked the conscientiousness and persistence to maintain the academic stamina required throughout the duration of college. The message for teachers is that those students who demonstrate the diver mentality in high school are headed for academic failure at college.

Self-descriptions provided by the students informed the researchers greatly. "Compared to the average student, divers were less likely to describe themselves as organized or detail-oriented, less likely to say that they are prepared, that they follow a schedule or that they get work down right away."[7] There is an interesting point to be made at this juncture for students in Gen Z.

Modern technology may be adding to greater levels of procrastination on the parts of the divers, whereas this same technology may be enhancing the ability of others to get right to work and accomplish deeper learning and better overall production, as may be the case with the thrivers.[8] Discounting the motivation, personality, and disposition of students is a mistake. The phrase that has been passed down from generation to generation apparently still contains wisdom for today: "A person can lead a horse to water, but he cannot make it drink."

The essence of being smart encompasses so much more than the utilization and application of user-friendly technology. In addition to what has already been presented, personality and various psychological aspects also come into play. Simple logic would draw the conclusion that a generation that assumes its smart technology makes a person smart must also admit that this must also apply to some Baby Boomers, Gen Xers, and Millennials who use the same technology.

Teachers in other generations possess high technological skills, far beyond pressing the "play" button on an ancient VCR. Would these skills force Gen Z to take notice of the smartness of teachers? If so, students would have to admit that some of those in previous generations may be equal or greater in technological literacy. There is nothing wrong with this. In fact, the generations will be working side by side in the tech trenches soon enough.

Being skilled in the use of smart technology is a good starting point for Gen Z students. However, there is more to smartness that should be considered. Those who thrive at college and consider their character a major facet of their smartness are more apt to describe themselves as "trustworthy, wise, helpful,"[9] what researchers refer to as "non-cognitive skills."[10] This is not the case with those whose academics plunge at college, where their focus was placed on the overall levels of difficulty of the work expected[11] or who were sidetracked by socializing. So the question must be asked, "What is literacy in the age of smart technology and who or what makes this determination?"

GEN Z AND DIGITAL LITERACY

Are teachers just fed up and need to vent or are they as bad as the students they criticize? Well, hacking into Slack, an app used by teachers, may provide some insight. As a colleague still in the trenches, there is hardly a day that goes by that I don't hear from teachers who are excoriated and denigrated by parents and students across social media. During and between classes, it is reported that students talk about what they "just posted" about this teacher or that teacher on Instagram and Twitter.

Twitter is used as a live feed from classrooms, and students interact with each other in 140 characters or less. Some students use Facetime and connect with others in classes until they are caught. These things occur while teachers are instructing. Daily social media posts and communication networking is much more a demonstration of negative literacy skills than positive skills. The exception to this may be digital video and audio production and blogging.

Creative use of symbols, emojis, emoticons, touchpad characters, and captioning and posting recordings may seem like there is an advancement of intelligence technologically. But is it really? On the negative side, teachers of Gen Z students must question whether these students are more literate because they have found new ways to circumvent instruction, bully and trash-talk, as well as hide things from others online. If the product is the assessment, then students are quite below basic in literacy skills.

Vindictiveness Is Not Smartness

If teachers only knew how often their photos appear online "doctored," they would be quite upset. Teachers' classes are being recorded without their knowledge and against their wills. In some states it is prosecutable to record someone without their knowledge, yet school districts and school administrators do little to combat the practice in schools.

Social network accounts have hundreds to thousands of posts daily criticizing teachers and schools, and some of these criticisms are quite vile and profane. However, not just students are involved in attempting to ruin teachers' reputations. Parents sometimes take to the Internet to vent anger and frustration about their child's teacher or school administrators. They are not *slack* about stepping in to fight on behalf of their children, even if it means demeaning other students.

Teachers are at a loss as to ways they can control students from ruining their reputations online by disparagement and ridicule and the use of profanity-laced insults. Some teachers fight back and post their own frustrations to try to settle scores once they discover what is taking place. Usually, this makes situations worse for the teachers. Parents call for these teachers to lose their jobs, while feeling what they post about teachers is within their freedom to express themselves. This is one argument for teachers staying off social media where parents and students troll.

Parents and students are always going to find ways to express their disenchantment. Students in Gen Z feel they are justified in posting what they feel at the moment. What Gen Z feels it immediately posts. Oneupmanship is emotionally gratifying. Posting online is horribly different from parking lot gossip or even passing notes in class. The audience is much larger online and the impact is immediate and possibly viral.[12] The last thing a teacher wants or needs is for a demeaning photo, a secretly recorded video, or a series of posts to go viral.

Awareness Cuts Both Ways

Abuse of teachers has become epidemic.[13] District-level administrators do not see these abuse-oriented posts, so they have no idea the degree or the extent of the abuse teachers take. Things may only get worse with the admission of newer and younger teachers to classrooms. Old habits die hard deaths. Adults who were raised to practice immediate gratification are going to have to learn self-control while they view what students and parents say about them in the digital realm. Would anyone be in favor of allowing teachers the latitude to rip into students and parents in fighting back at those who would sully their reputations? In other words, is it time to cut teachers some "slack" for ripping into their students?[14]

Students tend to think if teachers are not aware of what they do online that teachers are out of touch and that they are outsmarting their teachers. This is actually not the case. Teachers are becoming more aware of what is going on and some have taken to the Internet to complain about students and parents.

One recent Internet hack revealed exactly what teachers had been writing about students and their parents. As mentioned earlier, the hack occurred with the chat room Slack and teachers' chats were posted on social media sites. What was posted revealed that "teachers insulted students"[15] and then when they were caught, these same teachers "resigned in disgrace." Who can fault teachers for wanting to fight back? However, what Gen Z can get away with is not the same standard that applies to teachers. This might change with the influx of Gen Z college graduates entering the teaching profession.

Creative bullying online is not a sign of advanced intelligence. Teachers from previous generations must learn to reduce cyber bullying by taking better precautionary measures. Below are some practical suggestions that veteran and newer teachers may find helpful.[16] These suggestions should serve as points of beginning for teachers of Gen Z students.

Some Practical Suggestions

First and foremost, teachers must keep their private lives private. Often what is posted online is not private. If teachers are friends with their students' parents and they share time online with them, extra caution should be taken as to what is posted. Experience is a good teacher itself.

Second, when something is written about teachers online that crosses the line of appropriateness, these postings should be reported to school authorities. Print out what was posted and keep a record of these postings. Teachers beware; the first question that might be asked is "Are you also posting in that environment?"[17] There is often great difficulty defending oneself if a teacher has entered into the fray at times.

Third, it is advisable not to connect online with current and future students and their parents on social network sites. Adopting this policy will cut down on the amount of personal information that they know about you. The less people know about a teacher's personal life, the better. So keep personal relationships and photos about intimate details off the Internet. This should go without saying. However, we live in a climate in which the Internet is a person's immediate gratification fix of dopamine.

Last, there are other security measures a teacher could take, such as regularly changing one's password and doing regular Internet searches to see how and where his or her name is being used.[18] Students have access to affordable multifunctional devices that include "cell phones equipped with digital cameras and Web browsers that can play digital audio and video recordings . . . that readily support their interpersonal communication needs and multitasking behaviors."[19] In this Gen Z age of smart technology, if students feel smarter because they have secret knowledge that teachers are unaware of, then the challenge is for teachers to guard their lives like never before.

When Smartness Is Not Smartness

Gen Z students have a certain level of trust in what they read online. The vast numbers of students who get their daily headlines online are swayed by the glitz and professional appearance of what they read. Information that comes to them is not necessarily accurate. It is, however, optimized for their age and their interests online. At a time when fake news articles are in the headlines and revelations about Russian influences helping to shape an election, people cannot be faulted for doubting what they read. For all intents, who knows if the articles about fake news are not fake themselves?

Gen Z spends time online and has mastered the technique of copying and pasting links in order to complete assignments. One teacher brought chuckles to a room when she reported one of her students promised the work turned in was his work. He forgot to remove the URL link at the bottom of the page. Some students need a refresher course on how to define their work and work that belongs to others. Nevertheless, cutting corners with mastery does not result in increased intelligence—at least not the kind that will earn a student grades for which he or she can be proud.

There is an often misunderstood practice that is sometimes equated with higher intelligence. That is, there is an assumption that multitasking, the ability to process more than one task at a time, is evidence of advanced processing and great intelligence. Gen Z uses technology that does the multi-tasking, but one must question whether their brains are simultaneously capable of handling the tasks apart from their technology. In other words, are Gen Z students capable of thinking and processing while listening to music, reading a computer screen, doing homework, and a variety of other tasks?

The Myth of Multitasking

Researchers for the organization Children and Adults with Attention-Deficit/Hyperactivity Disorder (CHADD) have found that "what most people call multi-tasking is actually multi-switching."[20] People "switch back and forth between tasks so frequently that we think we are doing more than one thing at once, but we rarely are. . . . You can't type a text into your smartphone and read a school book at the same time."[21]

Students will claim they can consciously do more than one thing at a time when it comes to their schoolwork. However, such a claim discounts the reality that usually one or more things are happening *to* them while they are either focusing on something else or being distracted by multiple stimuli. A good example of this is when students claim to multitask while listening to music as they work. This is not multitasking. Certainly, the brain is performing many functions at once and senses are piqued. Multitasking with music would be consciously writing music or playing an instrument while constructing a written draft of an essay for a literature class. Again, something is happening to the students while they work. Maybe the myth of multitasking explains why some of the students' work teachers receive does not meet academic expectations.

A smartphone or a computer can have many apps or windows open at the same time. These apps and their files can run simultaneously and seamlessly. Some of these run in the foreground, while others open and run in the background. Machines do not have emotions and do not have human disabilities that interfere with central processing. If anything does go wrong with a machine, it is either fixed or discarded. The continuous shifting of students' emotions makes classrooms somewhat more difficult in management of learning and inhibit the overall class from being centered on the same goals on any given day.

Technology and Students' Emotions

Students who are highly impulsive or given to anger may find an increase of emotions while they are on their devices. Teachers have seen this escalation firsthand. Students and their parents must be made aware of the effects upon their children's emotions while they are connected technologically. Daniel Goleman explains how the brain tracks moods and emotions:

> Activity in the prefrontal cortex area alone tracks our moods: the right side activates when we are upset, the left when we are in good spirits. But even when we are in a neutral mood, the ratio of background activity in our right and left prefrontal areas is a remarkably accurate gauge of the range of emotions we typically experience. People with more right-side activity are particularly prone to down or upsetting moments, while those with more activity on the left generally have happier days. The good news here: our emotional thermostat does not seem to be fixed at birth. To be sure, each of us has an innate temperament that makes us more or less prone to happy or dour days. But even given that baseline, research links the kind of care we get as children

to our brain's capacity for joy in adulthood. Happiness thrives with resilience, the ability to overcome upsets and return to a calmer, happier state. There seems to be a direct link between stress resilience and that capacity for happiness.[22]

IS GEN Z SMART ENOUGH FOR LIFE?

Gen Z is graduating from high school and college, and the question arises, "Are they ready for the challenges that wait them?" By most accounts, Gen Z is as ready as any other generation was ready. However, consider that the United States is undergoing a radical shift in the way it does education. Readiness for college and the workplace was the buzz-phrase brought about by Common Core. High schools are graduating students in record numbers. So everything must be headed in the right direction. Not so fast!

The majority of college counselors are quick to point out that graduating from high school does not make an instantly ready college student. College professors are increasingly more appalled at the lack of skills students possess during their freshman year in college. They are appalled at the lack of writing skills, reading abilities, and overall literacy rates of comprehension.

High school counselors face ever-increasing pressure to find ways to graduate students. High school students, whenever they desire, can cease attending class, fall behind on purpose, and then be allowed by some high school districts to take one or more classes online or through contracted programs to make up credits in mere weeks in order to be eligible to graduate. Reiterating points made earlier in this chapter, such practices increase graduation numbers but do little to solve the problems that create the situation in the first place. Such solutions also do little to increase literacy and provide solid skills for college. The reality of many high schools is that many students who fail classes or cut school and fall behind are provided creative and alternative opportunities to ensure they graduate from high school on time.

Gen Z Education Paradigm Shift

Dual Enrollment. There is this practice gaining ground in American high schools that students may earn college credit by taking dual enrollment classes providing credits equivalent to junior college classes while still in high school. The same is happening with classes and programs in the trades, technology and coding, robotics and navigation, and hands-on skills classes.

Serious students can earn junior college credit while in high school, and there may be a nominal fee or no cost to them in dual enrollment courses.

MOOCs. Postsecondary students are able to enroll in college and take much of their program online. Some students enroll in MOOCs (massive open online courses) and need not matriculate in college or university in the conventional, traditional on-campus programs for all of their courses. In some cases, college degrees can be earned exclusively online. Universities are offering more and more complete programs this way in order to meet the needs of students and their schedules.

Gen Z students are outsmarting the traditional education paradigm and bucking the status quo directly from their dorms and homes. Traditional in-seat classes still exist and always will. There is truly no replacement for the actual in-person lecture. A close second is watching the same lecture via podcast or live streaming. Smart technology exists for students to find ways to accomplish academic programs in their way, all of which appeals to Gen Z.

Alternative Education Access. Technology and the Internet have provided students with alternative methods toward achieving their goals of undergraduate college education, additional training, or advanced degrees and certifications. The United States military also offers postsecondary programs and classes as incentives for recruits. Gen Z students might think there is greater technological intelligence in the ways they are able to accomplish education and extend their career choices, and that is fine. Variations in methods may well keep motivation high and interest piqued. The basis of these programs is user-friendliness. Gen Z is not the only generation to utilize these program offerings via this method.

Ordering books online, paying bills, replenishing debit cards, and shopping for items in general point toward Gen Z's technological savvy. However, this savvy is also shared with other generations who display a similar skill set. As more and more businesses and colleges transition programs to the Internet, this shift is increasing the intensity of online education as the beacon for every generation's points of access.

Given all these changes to education, earning college credit, and exploring new information, "Is Gen Z smarter than its technology?" The general answer is in the negative. Developing and programming, coding and creating content are areas in which Gen Z is competing with Millennials. Gen Z is extremely good at using the technology and especially good with applications for smartphones, but utility is only part of technological intelligence. In this sense, Gen Z is using technology more than Millennials and therefore has an edge in intellectual applications of technology over Gen X and other generations. But wasn't this something most already knew about Gen Z?

Gen Z and the Grand Experiment

Moving from high school to college is a rude awakening for some high school graduates. High school graduation is the major emphasis in schools today because it is a seriously weighted measure to evaluate high schools. At the college level, counselors point out that "high school grades have always been the single best predictor of college success."[23] Because there is no standardization or norming of grades from one high school to the next, using grades as the best predictor of success is experimental at best. Besides, most junior or community colleges accept almost everyone into their programs, regardless of grades.

This being the case, and record numbers of seniors graduating from America's high schools with lower literacy rates and lower reading and math levels, what are the implications of this reality for colleges? Michael Petrilli sums it up eloquently. He writes, "It's particularly urgent that those of us who support the Common Core be willing to speak honestly about these issues. If the new Common Core assessments set the high school graduation bar at true college readiness—meaning students are on track to take credit bearing courses from day one—the country is likely to learn that scarcely one-third of all students, and many fewer low-income students, are at that level now. Even Massachusetts, our shining star, gets just half its young people to that level."[24] Now this begs the question about how students are being graduated at record rates, a fact celebrated by the previous administration.[25]

Take, for example, the Gen Z student working as a cashier in a restaurant or a retail outlet. How many people have experienced the Gen Z student trying to figure out the change to return to a customer, especially when the register goes down? Are students really as smart as their technology or do they just trust it more? It is time to examine the premise a bit more closely.

SMART TECHNOLOGY AND THE TRUST FACTOR

Gen Z "students not only use technology heavily, they also trust it implicitly."[26] This trust can pose problems for students investing emotional energy into something or someone, which may only be real within perceptions. However, beyond perception, smartphones have excellent potential as cognitive tools among Gen Z students. If used correctly, they can enhance depth of learning and understanding. Hartman, Moskal, and Dziuban agree:

> From an institutional design perspective, we realize that knowing our students gives us many more options for engaging them in the learning process. Throughout the generations, colleges and universities have attempted to tailor instructional protocols to accommodate students' preferences for acquiring knowledge, enhance learning, recue ambivalence, facilitate maturation, and maximize success. The audacity with which the Net generation has burst on the academic scene has accelerated our need to understand its learning characteristics. A conundrum accompanies that solution, however: adaptation for the present generation may not be adequate for the next.[27]

Political and Social Action

Gen Z is quickly learning to use social media for the promotion of social causes. Social engineers and politicians know exactly what it takes to assemble a mob-like crowd in a flash. Flash mobs, crowd-sourcing for data, pleas for funding, quickly organized protests, assembling of large crowds for making political statements, and other efforts to raise social consciousness make it easy to utilize social media to get across a variety of platforms. Often what emerges is a lack of understanding why the masses are involved. They just have the perception they are important enough to add their presence and emotional support to the mix.

Gen Z is contacted more easily and consequently easier to manipulate because they consume most of their information and extend themselves in communication through mobile devices, such as the use of apps on smartphones and iPads.[28] Social media has been the medium of choice for Gen Z on issues ranging from treatment of animals, environmental concerns, and various social justice issues.[29] Good examples are the "Occupy Wall Street," "Same-Sex Marriage," and "Black Lives Matter" movements.

Presidential campaigns in the 2016 election cycle also took advantage of Gen Z's emotions by labeling people outside their parties as racists, crooks, mentally ill, and misogynists, as well as enablers and abusers. The shameful part is that the candidates themselves resorted to this rhetoric and name calling. Welcome to the new age of Twitter and social media candidacies.

Commercial Consciousness

The loyalty of reliability of Gen Z with brand name products in the marketplace is far less than the loyalties found in previous generations. There is a broader approach in the selection of items such as clothes, music, foods, games, and television programming. The purchase of quick gifts, fast clicking of stars for product ratings, and social media "likes" are right in the Gen Z wheelhouse. Many find it odd that vacations are planned based on customer star rating and gifts are avoided because of poor Yelp postings. Gen Z is directly in the center of the new digital commercial consciousness and it is on track to make one of the largest economic impacts on the economy ever measured for a generation.[30]

Mixing Ideologies

The desire to mix ideologies that appeal to their emotions, even if contrary to logic, parallels Gen Z's penchant toward being easily distracted and highly emotional. For example, Gen Z churchgoers might hear about traditional marriage and nuclear families from the pulpit, and their parents might reemphasize these ideas at home. However, Gen Z might "feel" deeply that no one should tell people whom they can love.

These sentiments would be posted online and eventually strengthened through social media with those likeminded. Some contend that such ideological mixing makes sense to Gen Z because emotions are their reality. There is difficulty in understanding this as Gen Z is supposedly closer to their parents' beliefs and interests than previous generations.[31] Teachers are dealing with this type of inconsistency daily.

Purposeful and Pragmatic

Gen Z is *cause-worthy* in the ways they look at the world due in large part to the emotional pleas made to them in schools and their exposure to behaviors modeled by those whom they idolize in secular culture. There are certainly social, cognitive, and noncognitive aspects to being purposeful. Smart technology allows social and cognitive connections. However, technology is not human and "you can't separate the cause of an emotion from the world of relationships—our social interactions are what drive our emotions."[32]

When the discussion about college and payment for higher education enters the conversation, Gen Z students seek alternatives to attending traditional college and search for other methods to pay for advanced learning because of the costs. Gen Z students, although said to place great value on college, are torn between their feelings about the overall value of the degree and the financial burden associated with it.[33] Gen Z is as pragmatic as they are purposeful. Hence, Bernie Sanders, a 2016 presidential candidate, hit the college cost issue squarely and attracted a host of Gen Z as well as younger Millennial supporters.[34]

The interactions in the digital world vary between generations, with Gen Z more inclined to have augmented reality and deeper interactions with people in the virtual realm, focusing on the speed at which these interactions occur. Website optimizers understand this well, knowing they have only a few seconds to impress upon someone to click the first interesting link they see. Gen Z tech habits are emerging as more pragmatic than the habits of Millennials and other previous generations.[35] A 2013 survey of some 1,200 Gen Z students ages thirteen to eighteen (2017's current high school and college graduates) bore out this conclusion. Wikia, "the world's leading collaborative media company and home to many of the Web's largest pop culture communities,"[36] released some very interesting survey data about Gen Z's smart technology habits.

Gen Z Is Smartly Connected

Five of the trends noted by the Wikia[37] survey include 1) 46 percent of Gen Z is connected online more than ten hours each day, 2) 73 percent of Gen Z surveyed reported that their connectivity begins within an hour of waking up from sleep, 3) more students are connected for greater lengths of time than were just months earlier, 4) 54 percent of students visit social media websites, including YouTube, for entertainment, as well as post their opinions and knowledge several times daily, and 5) 66 percent of survey respondents replied that their technology and connectedness make them feel like they can achieve things they once felt impossible. Just to show how things have changed, "YouTube users upload 60 hours of video per minute and they triggered more than 1 trillion playbacks in 2011." This triggering amounts to "roughly 140 videos per person on earth."[38]

Students are a bit more secure in finding answers to questions. However, they tend to gloss over depth for expediency. Teachers need to work around this reality. Gen Z students place their confidence for in-depth information in the hands of Internet optimizers and online traffic hounds. Clicking links as a "one-and-done" does not add much depth to students' understanding. Teachers should caution students that there might be a pseudo-security in which they invest. Factors of online data trust may have already developed as a norm for Gen Z, amounting to click-bait benefits for advertisers.

Gen Z is displaying shorter attention spans than previous generations. The brevity associated with Gen Z's attention span may exist because of the speed at which many Gen Z students can process a host of items. Hewlett-Packard technologist Alvaro Retana perceives some very concerning issues arising among Gen Z as he states: "The short attention spans resulting from the quick interactions will be detrimental to focusing on the harder problems, and we will probably see a stagnation in many areas, even social venues such as literature."[39]

According to Retana, all is not lost. But discipline is needed among Gen Z to press beyond their natural inclinations and into solutions for problems not associated with an Internet search or a video online. "The people who will strive and lead the charge will be the ones about to disconnect themselves to focus on specific problems."[40] Future employers also hope that Gen Z fights the tendency toward quickness and radiates the patience necessary to find solutions that extend beyond a quick Google search.

Faster Brains

Without a doubt, Gen Z has developed the edge with hand-eye coordination, a requirement for playing online games. This skill is an amazing thing to behold. Gamers play as teams and compete against others online, and Gen Z, along with some younger Millennials, is on the forefront of domestic and international competitions.

The number of commands sent to and from the brains of Gen Z are incredible in number. Gen Z brains tend to expedite more quickly, meaning their attention span is not as extended as other generations' attention spans.[41] The brains of gamers and prolonged uses of devices are wiring up rapidly firing neurons, accompanied by quick twitch responses. This set of connections enables Gen Z to find success at some things, but this success does not necessarily translate to success in the classroom—particularly in the areas of long-term memory development. Slowing down the brains of Gen Z is sometimes an insurmountable task for teachers.

Critical thinking takes time, and older generations seem to have this skill in greater numbers than Gen Z. However, Gen Z believes that circumventing time by using digital devices is expedient and more productive, therefore adding to the perception of greater benefit to their lives. Although counterintuitive, the time-tested axiom still holds true in telling students to *slow down and take their time.* There may be an even greater impetus for heeding this advice.

The more information that is accessible, the greater the need for digestion and assimilation. Sometimes speed in seeking information is a good thing for students. Other times, speed kills thinking and learning. Previous generations tend to focus on quality and depth. Whether their brains are better than those of previous generations is not clear. However, Gen Z could learn a lot from listening to the voices of others instead of only the sounds echoing forth from their devices.

Gen Z the Consumers

As consumers, a majority of students in Gen Z is apt to shop online rather than head to brick-and-mortar physical stores. The ease with which companies and brand names entice purchases and organize shipping plays directly into the psychology of Gen Z. They are anticipated to have a tremendous impact upon the American economy as consumers. According to U.S. census data from the 1990s, there are an estimated 60,000,000 members of Gen Z. This figure "outnumbers Millennials by at least a million people. They currently represent a quarter of the U.S. population [and] currently hold $44 billion in annual purchasing power in the U.S. alone. . . . Experts . . . attempting to tap into Generation Z will have to do so with pithy advertising . . . accustomed to emojis, hashtags and six-second . . . videos."[42]

Those brands seeking an inside avenue to marketing to Gen Z must take into consideration that the youngest members have barely begun elementary school. However, "their level of technological proficiency at such a young age . . . promises an almost unbridled capacity for digital fluency and innovation."[43] Gen Z approaches education as a consumer. They seek to consume in ways that fit their expectations. The question is, will education adapt to produce what the Gen Z consumer desires or will it go the way many brick-and-mortar retailers have gone?

CONCLUSION

This chapter began by asking the question whether Gen Z is smarter than their smart technology. The answer is a clear no. What Gen Z does, however, is use smart technology much more smartly than other generations. They spend more hours each day playing, communicating, socializing, and completing schoolwork. Therefore Gen Z's knowledge is wider and broader but not necessarily deeper. This is true whether discussing high school or college students.

The current education paradigm does not fit Gen Z. They prefer a consumer approach to education, with selections that fit their lives. Literacy rates are down, and there is some question as to why these rates are in contrast to the rising levels of high school graduation rates.

This chapter also addressed what it means to multitask and exploded the myth that Gen Z brains can actually focus on more than one task at a time. What is called multitasking by Gen Z is actually task switching because the human brain involves many facets associated with the ability to concentrate.

In closing, teachers are encouraged to delve more deeply into the ways smart technology can be used in the classroom to deepen student learning. Chapters 3 and 5 may be helpful for teachers seeking to provide such depth. Gen Z has so many wonderful traits about them. Teachers need to tap into these traits, expect excellence, and not settle for anything less.

Chapter Three

Teaching to Engage Gen Z

> Our education system produces solipsistic, self-contained selves whose only public commitment is an absence of commitment to a public, a common culture, a shared history. They are perfectly hollowed vessels, receptive and obedient, without any real obligations or devotions.[1]

Chapter 3 includes the following thirteen major sections: 1) changing roles of teachers of Gen Z, 2) neuroscience and Gen Z, 3) educational technology innovations, 4) teacher effectiveness with Gen Z, 5) strategies to assist Gen Z students' decision making, 6) connecting with Gen Z, 7) training teachers to work with Gen Z, 8) helping Gen Z learn by making brain connections, 9) Gen Z's future, 10) twelve tips for helping teachers work with Gen Z, 11) Gen Z as the first postliterate generation, 12) jobs for the future, and 13) conclusion.

CHANGING ROLES OF TEACHERS OF GEN Z

Education has undergone very radical changes over the last few decades. In many ways, schools have diminished their focus on a broad range of academics. Omitting the fine arts has detracted from student developmental balance and well-being. Schools have become the places of primary social services for students. To put it differently, "schools as we know them have existed for only a very short time historically: They are in themselves a vast social experiment."[2]

Curriculum and standards are being adopted in contrast to the beliefs of many American families. States are including learning standards that assert the benefits of lifestyles of groups that have in recent history run counter to the traditional customs and norms of the nuclear family. The role of the Gen Z teacher has now incorporated teaching content that may create disharmony in the classroom. Additionally, Gen Z college graduates entering the teaching profession will be more inclined toward social justice impacts and political change.[3] Teachers across generations will struggle on behalf of their generation as they move toward relinquishing the reins to Gen Z and the predicted influx of new teachers to occur.

Teachers now face the ubiquity of smartphones and the distractions that come along with them. Teachers have given up policing these distractions. Along with the changing roles of teachers, students also face many changes. Students need to adjust and modify their behaviors with technology if twenty-first-century American public schools are to focus on learning. Robert Earl illustrates this point:

> Students need more than just discipline in the classroom. They also need to be inspired to learn about the wonders of life, of humanity, of nature, of our planet, of the cosmos. School policies outlawing cell phones are clearly not enough—the effective teacher must connect with his or her students in order to hold their attention. There must be a magnetism, a bond between them, a sparking of a brotherhood in the battle for knowledge—a quest to figure things out, to understand, and to marvel and rejoice in that insight. . . . But the incessant cell phone use going on in our classrooms must serve as a challenge, forcing us to remember what education is really all about. The teacher's goal must be to instill an insatiable desire to learn.[4]

There were times in the past when teachers would respond to controversial or personal questions posed by students with the retort "Go ask your parents." Today such a response could pose one or more significant problems, given the state of some of the children and their living environments. Still, many parents bring their children to school with packaged expectations that schools are the places where students learn about everything from alternative lifestyles to how to behave, as well as establish proficiency in mathematics and language arts.

Today's teachers, probably more than ever in recent history, assume roles that cause them professional discomfort. Some take on these roles reluctantly, wondering whatever happened to the profession they love. Schools have become a major or essential place of stability in so many children's lives.

Aside from the teacher as teacher, classroom teachers have now become social case load overseers and academic managers.

In these roles as managers, teachers toggle between being a coach, counselor, and even a surrogate parent. Maybe it is the fact that most teachers at the elementary levels are female that some mothering type of aspect comes into play. Being married to an elementary teacher brings some reliable inside information. However, there is more to this story. Several teachers have shared with this author that with the continued rise of single-parent homes, they feel the need to step into the gap and support the students. However, they do so compassionately and reluctantly. Is it now the twenty-first-century teacher's role to parent his or her students?

In the upper grades, teachers act less as parents and more as coaches and counselors. The school as an institution, with activities and opportunities for various athletics and academics under coaches, provides much support for students, and assists them through mentoring and group-team dynamics. More and more public school parents expect schools to care for their children wholly and completely while they are at school. For too often teachers have heard the refrain, "That's the school's job."

Teachers, nearly as much as parents, struggle with meeting what they have been told are the "educational needs" of their students. Parents know it is impossible for teachers to meet the needs of their children. Nevertheless, twenty-first-century public education now encompasses a resurgent educational fad, which is being touted as the panacea for students and future workers in the global workforce. The fad is a comprehensive program called Social-Emotional Learning (SEL).[5] With SEL, there is the appearance that government schools are incorporating family-like traits and programs on behalf of American students. This only brings the reader back to the question as to whether schools are the places to mold children into social and emotional creatures.

Social-Emotional Learning (SEL)

Social-Emotional Learning (SEL) is a framework consisting of a network of stated core competencies for the twenty-first century. These skills include: 1) foundational literacies, 2) competencies, and 3) character qualities.[6] Foundational literacies focus on "how students apply core skills to everyday tasks."[7] Competencies hone in on "how students approach complex challenges."[8] Character qualities have their focus on "how students approach their changing environment."[9]

Within these three core competencies of SEL, students are expected to master some sixteen skills, ranging from mathematical and scientific literacy, to creative problem solving and collaboration, to curiosity and social and cultural awareness.[10] These are not separate entities in the learning environment. A student who is good at math and not good at collaborative problem solving to engage others toward excellence may well be viewed as weak in areas of the social and emotional bases. Therefore being excellent at math is not necessarily meeting the needs of the whole child.

This begs the question as to whether the Edisons, Einsteins, Gateses, and Jobses of the world would have made it in today's public schools. Conversely, some might ask whether exposure to public education with a corporate and all-encompassing SEL program might have resulted in even greater inventions and advances in theory and technology.

The Whole Child

An apology is offered here in advance (aka trigger warning), informing the reader of an attempt at humor. The title of this section evokes memories of a Dan Aykroyd *Saturday Night Live* skit focusing on the Bassomatic. Who can forget the famous line "Take the bass, the whole bass . . ." For the sake of extending the illustration, there is a high-speed blending that is taking place in public education. The last few decades in schools have brought about a definite shift requiring teachers to strive to meet the needs of their students under the guise of the philosophy of the "whole child." Education in academics is *much less pure today* and *much more psychological puree.*

Meeting the needs of students in their entirety is an impossible task. Yet teachers work within the realm of the impossible each day, acquiescing and enduring what their districts and administrators expect of them. The truth is that there is a great disconnect between expectations of districts and the realities of education. Rather than focusing on a few things, schools today expect all things to be in focus in schools, while easily distracted Gen Z students remain anywhere but at the center. In all candor, too many items moving in and out of focus make for distractions and confusion. Children cannot thrive in such an environment.

The "whole child" philosophy sounds very parental. The philosophy, by its definition, must also include the "spiritual needs" of children. Secular humanists maintain that the "human spirit" is where the needs are based, connected of course by emotions. Those of a faith background have a very different understanding of that which is spiritual and are reluctant for public education to approach students' needs in this area. Public schools have no place in engineering children toward social causes or elevating moral differences that are not held by their parents. Therefore, with these things in mind, public schools cannot and should not meet the corporate needs of all children, and here is why.

Meeting the needs of any one child at school is beyond reasonable. Asking teachers to meet the needs of thirty-five students in elementary schools and upward of two hundred students in junior highs and high schools—every day for nearly two hundred days—is absolute idealism and impractical. This is a nice attempt by ideologues within the disciplines of psychology and sociology to serve what they think are the best interests of children. Yet how many of these professionals have worked as teachers in schools before heading to the research institutes?

Depending of course on which political party is in power in Washington, DC, such notions probably make sense around the coffee pot, and even better sense if they can be funded by government grants and private foundations from those with similar ideologies. The program niceties sound quite caring to parents, and what parent would not like to hear that teachers and schools will love and care for their children as their own?

Twenty-first-century schools are in desperate need of more than engaging amygdalae through inquiry-based projects that flood students' brains with dopamine. Schools need to diversify the programs offered to Gen Z students. Today's skill sets require much more diversification and include high technology. At present, the SEL program comes with good intentions. However, if students do not transfer this learning into greater understanding while working on things that do not mine the depths of their emotions, then Gen Z might miss out on some very important twenty-first-century opportunities. The last thing we need is for students to fall farther behind while continuing to feel very good about themselves in the process.

Classroom teachers already know that learning is about the brain, and the more a teacher can involve students' emotions and passion centers, the more likely there will be a transfer of information into long-term memory. However, to base *all of learning* on the premise that through emotions children will always learn best is most presumptuous.

Immordino-Yang asserts:

> Scientific understanding of the influence of emotions on thinking and learning has undergone a major transformation in recent years. In particular, a revolution in neuroscience over the past two decades has overturned early notions

that emotions interfere with learning, revealing instead that emotion and cognition are supported by interdependent neural processes. It is literally neurobiologically impossible to build memories, engage complex thoughts or make meaningful decisions without emotion . . . emotions are skills—organized patterns of thoughts and behaviors that we actually construct in the moment and across our life spans to adaptively accommodate to various kinds of circumstances, including academic standards.[11]

Again, Immordino-Yang contends: "Emotions have evolved to keep us alive. Human beings have basic emotions, such as fear and disgust, to keep us off the edges of cliffs and to make us avoid spoiled food. We have social emotions such as love to make us affiliate, procreate, and care for our children. Thanks to our intelligent, plastic brain, we can also develop emotions that color and steer our intellectual and social endeavors, such as curiosity to make us explore and discover, admiration to make us emulate the virtue of others, and compassion, indignation, interest and 'flow.'"[12]

Immordino-Yang seems to envision a world in which everything learned is based in emotions and that is the result of emotional steering. Essentially, the end result is that the reality of anything learned is based in emotion. The implications of Immordino-Yang's assertions for teachers are important. With apologies to Rene Descartes, Immordino-Yang falls into "What I feel is therefore what I learned," and "What is not felt has therefore not really been learned."

Education today adds so very much to the classroom that can be mind-numbing. It places burdensome requirements on teachers. Many teachers are coming to the conclusion that the annual additional requirements are just not worth the energy any longer. Gen Z is being cheated in some ways. Today's education is beginning to look like it means less and less productivity is expected from more and more work. It also means less and less quality of learning due to the changing diversity of the classroom. Diversity has come to mean everything it has in the past, but with major medical concerns and psychological and learning issues added into the mix.

The fact is that today classrooms consist of diverse learners, serious brain-based learning disabilities, social and emotional problems, and behaviors that border on explosive and violent. The amazing truth is that even against seemingly impossible odds, the well-intentioned cohort remains in the game. They bravely march onward toward the expectations of improvement.

Where do we find ourselves as a nation in terms of reaching Gen Z? On the one hand, schools are expected to meet the needs of the whole child. On the other, teachers' hands are tied by the inability to meet the needs children have toward discipline in order to be successful.

Missing the Point

Education experts are missing out on one very important point. Teaching to engage Gen Z is as much about entertainment today as it is about giving in to the technological addictions and short attention spans. Increasing the expectations from teachers while lacking the understanding of the generation being taught is not producing anything of merit.

Teaching today's students must occur within a very limited window of focus compared to students of past decades. Some of this limited focus can be explained by the rapid shifts in what distracts students from important things. Teaching today's students also requires a very high level of energy and a modification of skills. Getting and holding the attention of Gen Z is a must, given the natural distractibility of today's students. However, having their attention for limited moments brings additional challenges. How then do teachers translate this attention into a form of learning and build a discernible cognitive schema worth assessing?

Today's Classroom

Education in America continues to focus on a past model in which classrooms were designed with the teacher as the center of attention. In terms of modern classrooms of the twenty-first century, knowledge and learning come to the students from several vantage points at one time.

Education has now flipped and what is learned outside the twenty-first-century classroom probably exceeds what is learned in a traditional classroom. Old paradigms die slow deaths and education paradigms live long lives. Although some of this learning may be insignificant and mundane, it is nevertheless learning. The weaving together and engagement of all of this learning, and for the Gen Z student steeped in social media, is best accomplished at the school with the teacher as the guide.

Both the teacher and the parent would do well to remember that Gen Z is not their generation. Technology for Gen Z has " blurred the lines of work and social, of study and entertainment, of private and public. Simplicity and flexibility amidst the complexity of busy lives are some of the key benefits that technology brings the digital integrator. They live in an open book environment—just a few clicks away from any information, they connect in a borderless world—across countries and cultures, and they communicate in a post-literate community where texts and tweets are brief, and where visuals and videos get the most cut-through."[13]

NEUROSCIENCE AND GEN Z

Neuroscientific discoveries have shown some promise in terms of suggesting methods that connect best with the brains of Gen Z students. Although not politically correct in their findings, most neuroscientists find there are stark differences between the brains of girls and boys. This reality brings with it the need for teachers to structure their lessons to meet the learning styles and brain wiring that exists among students. Teachers who accomplish this are doing a great service to the learner. Learners are benefiting from the learning when teachers teach to the styles of learning that naturally fit their styles of processing and understanding, as well as the fact that neuroscientists today contend that today's students' brains are wired differently than in the past.

There are major differences in the literature about what forms thinking. While it is accurate to posit that Gen Z thinks about many things and has to process a multitude of incoming data, there are differences in the ways brains form and explore ideas. One of the criticisms faced by Gen Z is that so much flies at them by choice that they are unable to filter the more substantive items upon which to reflect, which is actually much better for brains than fast-paced input. To this point, Jordan Cepelewicz clarifies:

> Early Homo sapiens wasn't acquainted with Einstein's general theory of relativity, yet anyone in a physics class today is expected to understand its basic tenets. "How is it that our ancient brains can learn sciences and represent abstract concepts?" asks Marcel Just, a neuroscientist at Carnegie Mellon University. In a study published in . . . *Psychological Science*, Just and his colleague Robert Mason found that thinking about physics prompts common brain-activation patterns and that these patterns are everyday neural capabilities—used for processing rhythm and sentence structure, for example—that were repurposed for learning abstract science. . . . "Everyone learns physics in different classrooms, with different teachers, at different rates . . . so it's surprising that the same brain regions are developed for understanding a physics concept in . . . students. . . . So even though some of these concepts have only been formalized in the past couple of centuries, our brains are already built to deal with them."[14]

The findings of a study by Just and Mason have serious implications for today's schools and teachers across disciplines. Classrooms compete for time. Some neuroscientists are quick to add to these implications, stating that "the findings may someday help determine which school lessons should be taught together for easiest consumption."[15] Imagine a classroom in which lessons are taught for students to consume the learning more easily!

Teachers can benefit from finding methods that convey to students the importance of taking the lead roles in their learning, both inside the classroom and outside the classroom. The benefit derived by teachers in students coming to this realization is the fact that students demonstrate skills and abilities that will enhance both their confidence and their performance. The development of character and skills will serve students well throughout the twenty-first century.

Donna Wilson agrees when she concludes: "Teaching students . . . they are the 'conductors of their own brains' conveys the need to master a wide range of thinking and learning tools for us across core academic subjects, in their personal lives, and later in their college years and careers. Success in the 21st century demands self-directed learners and independent, creative thinkers."[16]

EDUCATIONAL TECHNOLOGY INNOVATIONS

Teachers entering the ranks these days are probably more savvy and comfortable with technology and its educational uses in the classroom. Veteran teachers are often maligned for not stepping into the twenty-first century in terms of knowledge and utility of technology and the current generations whose daily diets consist of social media. For some teachers, technology is still a toy that is not worth the time to master.

Some of the innovations in social media platforms that remain popular with most Gen Z students[17] are usually found as apps on one or more of their devices. Table 3.1 includes many of these apps.[18]

When it comes down to the social media selections made by Gen Z, there is a departure in their selection in contrast to Millennials and Gen Xers. Gen Z students have watched the meltdowns and hits to reputations by their elders and decided to opt for something more private. Certainly to adults, the privacy of Gen Z can come across as consciously hiding something. That may be true. However, the Gen Z students' airing of all sorts of personal items and posting photos of the partying and suggestive sensual and sexual photos and

Table 3.1. Popular Gen Z apps

Snapchat	YouTube	Vimeo	WhatsApp
ooVoo	Jott	Yik Yak	Secret
Whisper	Popkey	Twitter	Instagram
Periscope	Facetime	Pinterest	WeChat
Messenger	Kik	Tumblr	LinkedIn

comments are understood to lead to the ruination of a career or will sully one's future.[19]

One of the things learned by Gen Z watching older generations dabble on the Internet is that once posted on the Internet, the digital realm is virtually forever. Gen Z has learned to adapt its use of the Internet and social media toward more privacy and is inclined toward posts that disappear from view in seconds, such as with Snapchat.[20] There is an element of caution that must be stated. Despite Gen Z's penchant for privacy, there is nothing truly private on the Internet. This should be reinforced regularly.

TEACHER EFFECTIVENESS WITH GEN Z

Teachers are always on the prowl for new strategies to enhance student learning. Prioritizing and managing time to do this can be daunting. For both the new teacher and the veteran, the consideration of basic priorities of classroom management, while working with Gen Z, can yield tangible effectiveness.

Priorities

Considering four priorities can lead to restructuring classroom management toward being more effective. In other words, how a teacher runs the show from beginning to end is critical. This includes first making certain all students comprehend the regimen set forth in the classroom. A second priority has to do with teachers reminding themselves daily that they are not teaching only material and content, but that they are teaching people. Therefore the building of appropriate relationships with students and families is another way to affect student success.

These relationships are points of connection that serve to enable student success both academically and personally.[21] Third, while navigating the classroom and tending to instruction, going with the flow is essential. Sometimes students take the lead and, as long as there is no major disruption to the learning, a few rabbit trails here and there are good diversions for the intensity of learning in many classrooms. The fourth and final consideration for teachers is the student behavior a teacher expects in his or her classroom.[22] These priorities should be communicated, reviewed regularly, and should become the mainstay of the standards of the classroom.[23]

Gen Z Student Decision Making

The next section includes helpful suggestions for assisting students in making executive connections and subsequent decisions in their brains.[24] There is one note for special education teachers, and that is that special education students may need varied approaches or differentiations and modification in what works best for them in the classroom. But this is not always the case.

STRATEGIES TO ASSIST GEN Z STUDENTS' DECISION MAKING

Students should be introduced to the concept of cognitive awareness. This awareness can lead to discovering the ways students' thoughts are applied to other decisions they make. This could be called application or extrapolation, reminiscent of several of the stages in the classic Bloom's taxonomy.

Examples of this transference can include students' choices to follow classroom rules and the comprehension of consequences. Conscious efforts are required by students as each transfers their learning. Teachers should model the actions expected by students and demonstrate the process the class is expected to undertake. This modeling is called the *executive function.*[25]

Second, teachers should provide opportunities for students to apply what they have learned. This would continue to keep the executive functions of the brain fired up. Minimizing distractions at this stage is important. Locking in authentic application of work should occur with minimal interruption. An example as to how teachers can accomplish this at all grade levels is by additional classroom readings on the topics at hand. Also helpful are classroom discussions to connect the learning and applications, challenging students to take on tasks or projects that lock in the learning by action and continued personal reflection about what students learned.

When students "get it," teachers should make certain to point out the connections and provide an emotional moment that extends the stimulation to the emotional center of the brain: the amygdalae. The chances are greater with Gen Z that learning will occur when students use emotions in concert with executive function.[26] What does this mean for teachers? It means that students learn best when their interests and passions are involved in the topic they are investigating.

Emotional reactions may be part of the learning. Teachers should remember the axiom "Practice makes perfect,"[27] and in building brain literacy—especially among elementary levels—more practice means more learning. The more myelin that lines the axons along the brain pathways, the better. The chances of emotional connections to what is being learned increase with application of material in relevance to students' lives. Application brings relevance and relevance produces connections.

CONNECTING WITH GEN Z

There are some tidbits to offer teachers seeking to understand the ways Gen Z prefers to connect with people. Without doubt these connections revolve around the world of technology and social networking. Teachers are encouraged to consider: 1) Computers are not just technology any longer. Computers are "an assumed part of life."[28] 2) Internet usage and online presence are far better for Gen Z when it comes to entertainment and socializing. 3) "Reality is no longer real."[29] So much can be changed online, and what is seen is not often what is actual. The digital world can be deceptive and surreal. 4) Gen Z enjoys learning by games and less by traditional methods. Teachers would do well to explore methods that make learning fun, engaging the interest of students and using technology to which gamers are accustomed. Today classroom learning for Gen Z "more closely resembles Nintendo than logic."[30] 5) Gen Z has grown up with the presumption that they have the ability to multitask. Listening to music, keyboarding, working in groups, and texting are simultaneities that could frustrate other generations. Not so for Gen Z. They self-proclaim that "multi-tasking is a way of life."[31] This self-proclamation is challenged in an earlier chapter of this book.

TRAINING TEACHERS TO WORK WITH GEN Z

There are significant differences in the brains of elementary school students, middle school students, and the students in high schools and colleges. Elementary school teachers are modern-day heroes. Twenty-first-century Gen Z elementary students are just as curious as students in the past. However, today's students in those grades are inherently much more distracted than in years past. Far too many stimuli come into the class with them, and what might have been called a distracted learner of the past may now be referred to as a student with processing concerns and attention disorders.

The training for public school teachers should include a hefty dose of brain development research and instructional strategies that can be implemented to connect new information to existing student schemata. The following basic realizations are those that teachers of Gen Z students will have to come to terms with early on in their training: 1) "Typing is preferred to handwriting, 2) Staying connected is essential, 3) There is zero tolerance for delays, and 4) Consumer and creator are blurring. The operative assumption is often that if something is digital, it is everyone's property."[32]

Both elementary and junior high teachers of today's Gen Z classrooms have particular challenges to overcome. These teachers must be able to switch their content focus much more quickly today, while holding the attention of their students. Students come to schools today with shorter attention spans and are very easily distracted. To coin a phrase, *elementary teachers today must strategically and purposefully distract the distractions of the students by being the more interesting of distractions*. The characteristics of Gen Z raise a host of questions for educators being trained by an older and possibly more entrenched veteran college faculty.[33]

Newer Teachers at a Disadvantage?

Newer teachers entering American schools may be at an initial disadvantage, particularly in four areas.[34] First, there is a lack of understanding of the different brains that are exposed to 24/7 technology. Second, teachers may be disadvantaged by the rampant narcissism of today's students. The "everyone receives a trophy" or "every student is an A student" in Gen Z describes just how easily a student's feeling could be harmed if left out.

Third, to what extent will teachers be able to practice honesty and empathy with the increasing inability to call out and correct poor behaviors or attitudes? Teachers must guard against being labeled or categorized pejoratively. Fourth, teachers should consider the ways they can use Gen Z's digital communication prowess to their advantage for student learning.

HELPING GEN Z LEARN BY MAKING BRAIN CONNECTIONS

Phil Parker, director of Student Coaching Ltd. in the United Kingdom, asked teachers to reflect on their understanding of Gen Z students:

> They are kids with brains rewired by the internet—answers to questions come from Google and YouTube, but they lack the critical-thinking skills to evaluate sources. According to Stanford University, this is freeing up brain capacity to develop such skills far earlier than previous generations. Gen Z are fast becoming the most successful problem-solving generation.
>
> Their brains have become wired to sophisticated, complex visual imagery. Audio and kinesthetic learning is out. So is talk—or lecturing as Gen Z sees it. They're avid gamers, they'll spend 30,000 hours gaming by the age of 20. They want learning to be the same: A sequence of challenges with instant feedback on progress, clear goals and rewards linked to them. . . . You want to engage Gen Z? Turn lessons into video games!
>
> Project-based learning in "flipped classrooms," where knowledge is explored at home and applied in lessons . . . has implications for the configuring of classroom furniture and technology . . . the shelf life of "knowledge" has never been shorter. The focus worldwide is shifting . . . to a process of gathering, analyzing and applying the knowledge . . . called "curating." . . . 1,250,000 teenagers manage their own website; they create a blog every second of the day. Gen Z wants to learn collaboratively and online. Best practice? Get them blogging and podcasting with other people, other schools.
>
> Pedagogical issues abound. Gen Z wants two things above all. Flexibility to learn in the way they find works best. . . . Gen Z mindsets are the focus of every forward-thinking nation . . . Gen Z are "digital integrators" . . . we can't teach them in analogue, where teachers do the teaching, spoon-feeding them knowledge. Those days are gone.[35]

Teachers have a lot to process in order to be successful each day in the classroom with Gen Z. The extent of success with Gen Z will depend on the measures of teacher and student flexibility they are willing to express and tolerate.

GEN Z'S FUTURE

What new directions will schools and teachers take to accommodate Gen Z?[36] Teachers and administrators must consider, "What does this mean in the schools and the classrooms?"[37] Teachers must be flexible enough to undergo yet another set of changes. They have already endured the murkiness of

Common Core, the implementation of ESSA, as well as the newest generation of students who are the guinea pigs amid both.[38] Through it all, teachers are now aware that Gen Z students come hard wired with high-tech classroom expectations.[39]

Colleges are making every effort to predict the shape of teacher education for the next decade. They have done so with an influx of the newest generation of students, including those from other nations. Some of these students will become teachers, making efforts to reach back into their generation to make a difference.[40] Some states' teacher-training institutions are holding firm in training students with Common Core methods. The political implications are many, and education always seems to be caught in the middle. So the nation shall have to wait to see which direction education policy heads under the Trump administration. The essential question is, what will be the state of education with Gen Z, given the fuzzy future?[41]

Suggestions for teachers to leverage Gen Z's affinity for technology:[42]

- Use technology's immediate feedback to motivate students and increase their learning confidence. Games are helpful in this area.
- Plan projects and activities that allow students to collaborate online. Blogging, podcasting, and digital media are some of the new tools that allow students to connect with each other and with other students around the world.
- Take advantage of Generation Z's increased visual learning ability by enhancing lectures with film, PowerPoint presentations, and digital images.
- Help students develop critical thinking and problem-solving skills, especially with their use of technology.
- Train students to focus their attention on a single task that has depth and complexity.
- Encourage students to set aside time for outdoor physical activity. Expedition Learning (EL) is an excellent way to connect reality and the virtual world.

TWELVE TIPS FOR HELPING TEACHERS WORK WITH GEN Z

In what ways can teachers of all generations become more helpful to Gen Z? Gen Z is the generation that spends more time using Snapchat and watching YouTube videos than it does watching any network or cable television. Gen

Z grew up with computers and smartphones.[43] The ironic part about Gen Z's technology and their usage is that many of them do not even know what "www" or "http" means or what dot-com stands for. Gen Z has some gaps in their knowledge.

Tip #1: Teachers who will eventually enter the teaching profession from Gen Z will need veteran mentors. These mentors will be required to assist the newer teachers in transitioning from a high percentage of reliance on technology to a balance of educational and personal utilities. Although technology is making definite strides to replace aspects of traditional education, education is still about people and will remain so for some years to come. There are concerns that veteran teachers are leaving the profession in large numbers due to Common Core and the lack of support by administrators. Veteran teachers are the gold standard and are the stalwarts in connecting the past with the present.[44] Newer teachers are encouraged to seek out veterans and learn from them.

Tip #2: Become technologically literate. Teachers should strive to incorporate whatever technology is available to them and their classroom to enhance learning. Request school- or district-level educational technology training and utilize this training to enhance lessons. Grants are available for schools and local districts. The George Lucas Educational Foundation has grants listed on their website: https://www.edutopia.org/grants-and-resources.

Consider that the average attention span for a Gen Z student is anywhere between eight and fifteen seconds. This can be a real concern for those teachers who choose lecture as their primary means of classroom instruction. Gen Z students are self-directed learners and will complete tasks when they see relevance. They also "prefer active learning and a student centered environment."[45] With these things in mind, high schools and colleges will find Gen Z students losing interest in lectures. Their brains are wired differently and they appear soft and lazy. They will disconnect and demonstrate this disconnection when they sit in class with one ear bud plugged in, listening to music. Technological literacy for teachers will generate new ideas to help reshape classroom instruction. Education is not just about changes, but changes for the better.

Tip #3: Realize that Gen Z has been reared with fewer restraints. Some of the behaviors they practice that garner attention in class are merely expressions of their student-centric world. Teachers are going to have to develop manageable policies and procedures to keep classroom management concerns to a minimum. Every teacher faces this dilemma in terms of what policies to establish and uphold.

Teachers in elementary schools are becoming more and more frustrated as they complain that students have less and less self-control, are allowed to disobey adults with impunity, and are "mouthy" and disrespectful toward those in authority. Teachers will often learn much more about student behavior once they meet the parents of their students.

Gen Z students come with recreational mindsets. School has become, for some, a place to play at life. Because playing is supposed to be fun, students expect some semblance of fun in classes. For most of the students' lives, participation counts as involvement. That is, everyone should get an "A," like they all get certificates or trophies for participating in events. Who can blame them?

High schools are graduating more students with fewer skills, much less knowledge, and lower reading and mathematical literacy rates. Diplomas are feel-good tools these days, and to restrict anyone from getting one—even if not earned—would be mean-spirited. Teachers should realize that education is now all about the students, while at the same time finding ways to recapture some of the teacher focus for the sake of balance.

Tip #4: Classroom management for teachers of Generation Z can be quite frustrating. One of the reasons Gen Z students may distract others or find themselves in the midst of classroom discipline is the result of boredom. "Good classroom management is more than just being strict or authoritarian, and it is more than simply being organized."[46] Classroom management is directly tied to setting up a "structured learning environment in which certain behaviors are promoted and others are discouraged."[47] Students will seize the opportunity to flourish if they know the teacher cares and achieves the "most important component of classroom management,"[48] which is the building of relationships.

Student Impatience. Gen Z does not have the patience to wait for many things—not the least of which is finding answers and arriving at thought-out solutions. One of the better ways to avoid the boredom of Gen Z students in the classroom is to provide educational freedom for students to explore topics of their own interest and allow them to connect their interests to everyday life.[49] However, students need to be made aware that teachers do not expect them to master material immediately and that direct access to information or answers to questions is not the same as mastery.[50] Gen Z students expect to learn things quickly, otherwise they are bored, give up, and move on. Technology has afforded quickness as a substitute for substance and depth. It is the teacher's job in every classroom to slow down the search for worksheet answers and cultivate deeper learning through relevance and life applications.

Develop Policies. Students will be distracted and continue to check their cell phones and even take phone calls during class. Develop a set of policies that place classroom learning first for all students. A teacher who allows a precedent for students to use their phones as their impulses direct will find it difficult to maintain classroom decorum. On a personal note, classroom rules that minimize cell phone distractions are difficult to maintain without a school-wide policy.

Teachers in other classes that allow unlimited use of cell phones and access to them during lessons and group work make it increasingly difficult for other teachers to hold students accountable for behaviors and learning in other classes. Such distractions detract from the overall learning environment and should be monitored closely. Likewise, teachers who are using their cell phones in class add to the distractibility of students at all levels and set a poor precedent for learning. There is another very important aspect to allowing cell phones in the classroom and it comes with unintended consequences.

Teacher Evaluations. Cell phone distractions that occur in classrooms in which teachers are being evaluated officially in order to remain employed or to advance in the profession can often work against the teacher. As a professional, this policy appears to be completely unfair, especially in school districts where there is wide-open classroom access to smartphones on campus and in classrooms. Administrators should not hold teachers accountable for students in classes who are using their cell phones at the wrong times. This is much more than a classroom management issue. This is a school culture issue, and one probably established by a principal or district-level administrator.

Student Addiction. As a reminder, Gen Z is addicted to their devices and students come to class with temptation tugging and compulsion calling every few seconds. "Teachers can receive poor ratings from their Assistant Principals if students are not paying attention to teaching because they are texting."[51] This is most unfair because teachers cannot ban cell phones from their classrooms. For example, high schools across the nation are reporting that teachers are stopping instruction several times during each class period "to reprimand students for using their cell phones,"[52] often leading to confrontations and major distractions in the learning environment.

If teachers cannot command the attention of students and then are penalized for this, it is most unfair to the teachers. In fact, if students are off task habitually because of disobedience in using their smartphones, should they be penalized in their grade for that class? Psychologists and special education experts would argue that is not fair to students who are *not* addicted to their devices, but then want schools to offer assistance for the addiction. They also have a point.

Smart Technology Policy. The world of smart technology can sometimes make education appear that there is nothing left but hopelessness and that smartphones are adding to this hopelessness. Certainly, schools and districts have to do much better at setting policy. Likewise, colleges and universities that are training the next generation of teachers have to make certain that teachers from Gen Z itself understand when and how to use smartphones. This would mean that newer teachers would either give in to their device addictions or modify their behaviors and classroom practices for the benefit of their students.

All things considered, teachers should recognize the appropriate moments to use smart technology in the classroom and should not be fearful of disciplining students who simply disobey and become distractions to the overall learning environment. Just because Gen Z is the wired up generation does not give them carte blanche to use the technology as they please in the moment they choose, especially to interrupt classroom learning or disobey in class. Giving in to this sense of compulsion on the parts of Gen Z means that their technology has become what educational researchers refer to as "time stealers."[53] Teachers in these cases must become *time redeemers*.

Tip #5: Remind yourself that student self-esteem and self-perception are paramount among students of Gen Z. Gen Z is easily offended and often lead into experiences with their emotions. Veteran teachers must be keen to cultural changes in America. Using language that avoids inflammatory meanings and diminishes upset over issues that are significant to Gen Z students is the mark of a teacher who has a wide vocabulary. Be careful not to offend the easily offended students, but also instruct them that the real world cares little about how they feel about their emotional reactions.

Using Humor. Today's teachers should allow themselves opportunities to demonstrate humor and a spirit of fun as they instruct classes and work with students. Professionals working with young minds should guard against using satire, sarcasm, and cynicism as substitutes for humor. Therefore engaging students with humor should come with some guidelines.

Ted Powers provides several guidelines to engage students with humor.[54] These include four basic guidelines to remember: 1) Teachers should guard against hurtful or offensive humor. Today's generation is quite soft and feels things that sometimes are not meant by the persons sharing the humor. 2) Teachers should be aware of the makeup of the students in their classes and be mindful that some humor might reopen old wounds in some students. This has prompted the phenomenon of *trigger warnings* across college campuses. 3) The tone of voice and the intent of the humor are equally important. At this point sarcasm as humor might have a tendency to creep in. Be on guard not to establish sarcasm as classroom decorum. 4) Humor should be relevant, genuine, and applicable to learning contexts. Include some self-deprecation so students see it is all right to be human.

Using the Internet. The use of YouTube and short online vignettes can enhance the classroom atmosphere and the learning environment. "By linking course information to popular, fun shows you show students that course concepts exist in the real world in which they live."[55] Every student likes to have fun. Injecting humor to make learning fun for students often makes teaching fun for teachers. Humor is a tool that all teachers should strive to implement.

Humor is also an avenue that touches emotional centers of the brain. Heartfelt laughter and relaxed moments of humorous learning travel their course through the brains of students and thereby embed themselves, usually easily recalled long after the day ends. Students talk a lot about fun classes and fun teachers. They also talk about other classes that are not so much fun. They use terms such as "boring" to complain about classes that do not excite them.

Relationships Are Key. Teachers of Gen Z students must never underestimate the extent that relationships develop in the classroom. Technology allows these to develop and flourish, often without face-to-face interaction, which can sometimes be too risky for some of the more insecure students in Gen Z. By comparison, Gen Z students are fearful of risk taking and do not have the same level of confidence that even the Millennials possess.[56]

Gen Z relies far too much on the Internet and social media for relationship security. Gen Z, even with their reputation for impulsivity, should take time to develop the security required to make certain life decisions. Google does not have this function figured out yet. Remember, parents are still heavily involved in the decision making of their children. Teachers should be reminded of the fragile nature of the emotions and psyches of today's Gen Z students.

Tip #6: Develop lesson plans that are challenging and in-depth research with some focusing on inquiry-based units. Gen Z likes to think and explore for answers. Inquiry-based research projects, discussions that require several levels of conceptual statements, logical premises and conclusions, and a host of other lesson types are enjoyable to Gen Z students. These kinds of challenges will take time to develop and Gen Z must be trained to face such challenges.

At first, it appears counterintuitive to state that lengthy and challenging lessons fit the nature of the Gen Z student. But it is true. Students love to learn and enjoy the self-discovery over being told what to do and how to do it. So more self-discovery and less lecture is one good way to engage Gen Z toward the goal of deeper learning. Gen Z students are *educational entrepreneurs* when it comes to *taking research risks in search of how it can profit them.*

Tip #7: Thwart the tendency to return to the assessment types administered under NCLB and even Common Core. Gen Z is burned out on those "bubble" assessments. The assessments using the computers today are like the Common Core bubble types, and students get bored reading long passages of text. Students do not read with the same critical eye like they used to read. No longer are they required to delve deeply into the classics. Today's literature classes are favoring shorter nonfiction articles for their students. Of course, bubble-type assessments are the easiest for the teacher to grade, but they do not tell the teacher much of anything in terms of what students truly learned.

On a personal note, there is the recollection of one student who edited an English essay in a most interesting way. This is a pure example of a Gen Z student in action. The student opened the essay on his cell phone via a document in the cloud and used an app to edit the piece. He accomplished this during his lunch, while he was seated on a cement planter. The student then downloaded it in a classroom and opened the document in a word processing program on a laptop. Within minutes, the document was then printed and ready to turn in for credit. All of this was done on time as an assignment and given full credit.

Check with Colleagues. Teachers can find ways to be creative and borrow other teachers' ideas to enhance their classroom techniques. Google Classroom, Google Docs, and other school-friendly programs are rapidly becoming teachers' and students' best online academic tools. The tech-savvy Gen Z entrepreneur finds ways to be academically successful. Teachers of Gen Z must become proficient in the technology used by their students.

Tip #8: Remember that beginning in 2017, education policies and regulations at the federal and state levels changed again. Moving from a one-size-fits-all Common Core philosophy to one that is more local will bring with it many changes and challenges. Policy regulators always have the final say about which elements of education programs address one issue or another. With the shift under ESSA, teachers should be aware that Gen Z students may be confused in determining some of their educational direction for the duration of their K–12 experience. This confusion can either be clarified or compounded with the addition of Career Technical Education (CTE).

Tip #9: Understand that ELL, ESL, ELD, bilingual students, special needs students, and special education classified students are also part of Gen Z. Many of the students presently in special education programs will be mainstreamed and assessed under ESSA. Likewise, states are going to be determining what levels of funding and which programs will be strategic to tackling bilingual education and various special education programs. The federal government is especially concerned that under ESSA some states will spend less than others on education. Those in favor of increased spending have lobbied to include a near "one-size-fits-all" dollar expenditure, regardless of the state and the educational programs. This has become known as *supplement, not supplant.*

Teacher training institutions are adding classes concerning special education methods for teachers in order to *"teach and reach"* these students more adequately. The numbers of students in these categories is growing each year. The numbers of teachers required to fill the classrooms across the nation are also going up. Some states are realizing teacher shortfalls for one reason or another. There is no doubt that with the emergence of Gen Z, teacher training has taken on new courses to prepare the newest generation of teachers for what is to come.

Tip #10. Harness the human capital of Gen Z to accelerate learning and provide several educational options for students to complete their programs off site. This works especially well for high schoolers. One of the latest creative educational nuances is an approach that actually competes with Advanced Placement classes at the secondary level. The approach involves junior and/or community colleges partnering with high schools to offer students the challenge of dual enrollment. Students, while in high school, can actually earn college credit on their transcripts, making their stay at college shorter. It is a nice option and should be expanded to more disciplines and skill areas.

Other students are taking Career Technical Education classes and learning robotics and coding and taking other science/technology classes online. Occupation centers are training students to be ready to join the workforce directly out of high school. Students are coming out of elementary and junior highs and entering secondary schools with much more technological capital than in the past. Gen Z's tech skills are growing and there must be opportunities available to them so they can flourish.

Tip #11: Whatever the grade level teachers are assigned, they should have a working knowledge of Gen Z students' emotions and expectations. Gen Z is passionate about their technology. They are also passionate about getting what they want. As desirous as they are, Gen Z is also highly impatient.[57] Sometimes students use the strategies and manipulative ploys they have learned from their Millennial and Gen X parents in terms of getting what they desire. This desire includes moving students from one classroom to another because of small issues.

Gen Z is less about principles and more about emotion. Of course, these are generalizations based on anecdotes and observations by educators. These are not characteristics of every Gen Z student. However, "As more generations come into the workforce, the focus is starting to shift from the year they were born to the characteristics they deliver."[58] Gen Z is beginning to affect American culture, and they seriously expect to accomplish this. Teachers can help shape the future by contributing to the development of students in the present. Such can be a legacy of any classroom teacher.

Tip #12: Parents of Gen Z students have no problem going directly above people's heads to change something or using technology to complain and get their way. Parents can be the very best advocates for classroom teachers. Teachers must be aware of the nature of this advocacy today. A shift in interpersonal approaches needs to be considered with adults whose children are from Gen Z. Newer teachers who will eventually make their ways into America's classrooms will view life differently than those of veteran status. Younger teachers find it easier to criticize a colleague on their social media pages. Parents have little problem sharing their concerns on these same Internet pages. Students join in and find it easy to use texting, post photos to Instagram, or vent on Twitter. Many who resort to venting on the Internet can now be called *hyper-gripers*.

Teachers can help themselves immensely if they remember that they "tend to focus on the Internet as a source of content or information . . . encouraged to design assignments that foster the Internet as a communication and teaching tool . . . in the new digital environment."[59]

One reason to steer clear of participating with parents and students online is that Gen Z students and their parents use immediate action to state their opinions, usually going around or above the person/persons in authority. Bullying has become the catchword of this generation. Social media are used to harm and even ruin adults and fellow students. Rest assured, any teacher or professor who works with students probably has had his or her photo posted on a student's page, some personal or professional photos or social media posts copied and pasted, or has been the subject of an in-class texting charade.

GEN Z AS THE FIRST POSTLITERATE GENERATION

Gen Z is the first postliterate generation. This means that students in schools do not need to craft their own words or assemble their own research to analyze and synthesize data. This is all done for them by means of software, online websites, and applications. Figuring out light angles and apertures for photography are no longer requirements for taking good photographs in the digital age. Smartphones and expensive digital cameras do all the figuring. Cash registers in stores do the processing, and thinking is secondary, which means it is no longer a prerequisite. In terms of Gen Z students, obedience to the technology at hand is the prerequisite that is necessary for success in school and in most workplaces.

Gen Z students have never truly "engaged in formal exercises comparing advantages, disadvantages, strengths, and weaknesses of the Web with other informational tools such as books and print journals. Members of other generations are more likely to use this sort of mental comparison automatically, only because they have had more experience with the different types of research tools."[60]

The fact that Gen Z students rush to Google to find their answers for many questions implies that they are not persistent in approaching even the most remote consideration of exhaustive research on a topic. If it cannot be found within a few seconds and clicked, Gen Z students move on. "They often do not have the metacognitive skills to know when to stop using Google and other search tools and to try a different information search strategy."[61] Gen Z would much rather watch a short video and then apply the skills required to solve a problem.

One of the selling points of Social-Emotional Learning is its aim to improve students' literacy skills across academic domains and enable students to develop packages of skills to ready them for the changing twenty-first-century workplace. However, is this the right approach? The increase of technology and the distance it naturally places between people do not bode well for the future of programs that intend to bring people together face to face in social and emotional ways. Students are learning to communicate in short videos that amount to less than ten seconds and by ways of text, where brevity and emoticons, bitmojis, and emojis are the rule. In order for social and emotional learning to make any difference, students have to learn skills counter to how they socialize and currently communicate.

JOBS FOR THE FUTURE

Basically, SEL proclaims to focus students on skills that are fashioned as necessary for jobs that do not yet exist. In fact, some of these hypothetical jobs may not come into the picture until at least the year 2030.[62] Literacy skills for Gen Z are meant to transfer to all students and in all schools on a grand, global scale as part of the social and emotional learning model put forth by the March 2016 report of the World Economic Forum.[63]

Harvard professor David Deming writes that "learning must be transformed in ways that will enable students to acquire the broad set of skills that will help them thrive in a rapidly evolving, technology-saturated world."[64] But is SEL to be included in this transformation and skill acquisition, given the prediction that people will work in greater capacity with technology? Something is missing in this economic forecast.

In some ways, the resurgence of SEL is a type of Common Core for social and emotional skills. Common Core is all but washed up as national educational paradigms go. SEL may follow the same path, given the fact that the program itself boasts "investors put $440 million into companies designing programmes to track, assess and improve student performance and outcomes, mainly those that emphasize foundational literacies and Common Core Standards."[65] Now that many states are continuing to distance themselves from the toxicity of Common Core, the Every Student Succeeds Act (ESSA) will determine the newest direction for education in the twenty-first century. The empowerment of local communities, once again, may result in emotional displays, this time of levels unpredicted.

CONCLUSION

The Gen Z learner brings some unique challenges into the classrooms of America. Teachers would do well to seek out professional development in the areas of modern technologies. The old days of analog and monochrome are long gone. The greater the gulf between the teacher's knowledge of technology and students of the digital age, the greater the frustration when students disregard directions and the less the teachers will appreciate the way the brains of Gen Z are wired.

Without additional training in technology and in the ways Gen Z learns with this technology, many teachers will be placed at great disadvantage. They will be unable to both understand their students' styles of learning and take advantage of their technology for the sake of learning.[66] Teachers who wish to engage Gen Z learners should take note of the characteristics that make up the character of the learner.

Teachers should not make the mistake that all Gen Z students are experts in technology. The copy and paste mode of research draws attention to the fact that Gen Z is not savvy when it comes to using others' intellectual property. They still have much to learn about their devices. Moments to teach ethics abound for those working with Gen Z.

Because the brains of the Gen Z learners are wired for speed, it is natural that rapid sourcing of data would occur. Gen Z brains appear wired to input information as quickly as possible. One of the hazards of this is the lack of desire and even inability to check on the validity of the information being rapidly processed.[67] In this sense, speed kills depth of learning. Another concern is the lack of risk-taking employed by Gen Z. The unknown is challenging to Gen Z which, for many, probably stems from being culturally coddled toward a personally ingrained sense of entitlement.[68] Teachers should press Gen Z into efforts that require risk, even if it means they fall short and receive no prize from their risk taking. This is, after all, patterned after the real world. Millennials understand this. Gen Z has a way to go before it truly grasps this reality.

Gen Z students should be prodded to adopt a lifelong learner philosophy rather than a snippet approach that maintains an "I found the answer to life's questions online."[69] Methods to accomplish the first steps toward lifelong learning include 1) instructing students to question material and pose skeptical queries in order to dig more deeply into what is being studied. 2) The use of current events to encourage students' interest to delve deeper into a topic. In this way, students would be prompted to explore different areas connected to the current event. 3) Encouraging students to be curious while at home. Practice a flipped classroom model in which students research a topic at home and incorporate what they have learned into the lessons on the next day or subsequent days.

There is a misnomer that has persisted in education for several decades. This misnomer is as untrue today as it was when schools began to be the comprehensive social institutions they are today. Some bureaucrats, politicians, and educrats truly believe that schools are the places where society meets all the needs of children. The mission that "schools have to meet the needs of all students and the whole child, not part of the child"[70] has appeared as a school motto for decades.

The practices have followed the progressive belief that in meeting the needs of the whole child, schools are actually meeting the extreme needs of the few. For example, not every child needs a place to vent or to learn mystical breathing exercises taken from an eastern religion. Yet schools still maintain "strategies to bolster social and emotional skills include class meetings, breathing exercises, individual check-ins and safe spaces where students can go to calm down without feeling like they're being punished."[71]

The truth is that schools cannot meet all the needs of students and cannot meet the needs of the whole child. For example, if parents raise their children to ponder deeper spiritual questions of faith and God, schools do not veer into that area to meet the needs of the "whole" child. They are more reluctant to do so today, especially with those whose faith traditions were an integral part of our nation's founding. Political correctness has run amok.

Schools have become places of counseling, safe spaces for allies of lifestyles and practices, institutions of multiple chances, and discipline-free zones, as well as places to learn and thrive. The latter is sometimes squeezed to a minimum for the sake of the din of clamoring voices for social action. No one person has the capacity to meet the daily needs of any person, let alone focus on an institution tackling hundreds to thousands of "whole persons" each and every day. Schools should stop trying to do the impossible and focus on the achievable and the sustainable. If schools do this, they become an authentic partner with each student as they assist him or her toward realization of success in meeting life's goals.

Chapter Four

Expectations of Gen Z Students

> Well, who are you? (who are you? who, who, who, who?) I really wanna know (who are you? who, who, who, who?) Tell me, who are you? (who are you? who, who, who, who?) 'Cause I really wanna know (who are you? who, who, who, who?)
>
> —"Who Are You," The Who

Chapter 4 includes the following nine major sections: 1) identity is everything, 2) feelings are the new identity, 3) everyone gets a trophy and a free lunch, 4) not everyone is protected, 5) student-centered schools, 6) a rude awakening: Gen Z in the marketplace, 7) Gen Z and economics, 8) the fuzzy future of Gen Z, and 9) conclusion: Gen Z's feelings on issues.

There is an old saying, "As California goes, so goes the nation." The nation's largest state has some sway, and its impact is particularly pertinent in the areas of social, political, and educational agenda. Those who have made a name for themselves in media and entertainment or hold a stake in these high-profile arenas are often on the cutting edge of change.

California's statewide progressive political elite have a direct impact upon education. New York, New Jersey, Illinois, and several other states with very high concentrations of liberal voters celebrate the largesse of government oversight and state programs. These states and others are not shy about celebrating their political identity as it translates into economic, educational, or electoral successes.

IDENTITY IS EVERYTHING

The last decade has seen a rise in marginalized group empowerment and concerted efforts toward social justice. Unfortunately, these efforts have also led to shaming others, often in the majority, who disagree on social or political grounds. Today the nation is experiencing a newer set of challenges. One of these challenges has risen in conjunction with social empowerment. Self-worship has developed into near-religious fanaticism, and Gen Z is swept up in the fervor.

Political correctness has joined forces with identity politics. The result of this alignment has revealed a darker side to American culture. Our nation is more deeply marginalized and personal empowerment has led to greater divisions across many demographic lines. Gen Z is directly in the crosshairs of this cultural division.

The time-honored and hallowed right to express oneself has fallen subject to the political forces that find even disagreements unacceptable and intolerable. Those who shouted unfairness in the past are today practicing similar unfairness themselves. They do so with the force of progressive legislation on their side in many states.

Accentuation of the Divide

Working in education today accentuates America's social divide. Twenty-first-century American students are subject to cultural forces at schools and in communities at large. They cannot escape the reality of identity politics and the movement that has caused its outgrowth.

The 2016 presidential election of Donald Trump promised to bring new changes to our nation's identity. There was the promise to challenge the divide that existed at the time of the election. The result of this rhetoric was additional marginalization and divisiveness. People sense a power shift and groups empowered for nearly eight years are voicing their disenchantment with the possibility of the empowerment of counter groups, likely more conservative politically and socially.

As our nation moves through the remaining years of the decade, one can be certain that there will be identity clashes in culture and each clash will manifest itself in America's public schools. The emotional makeup of Gen Z makes it ripe for involvement in such clashes.

Students naturally take sides and this played out quite volubly in classrooms all over America during the last election. The truth is that empowerment of groups on one political side emboldens groups on the other. The slipping away of power is not an easy proposition with which to come to terms. Gen Z may be heard proposing, "Why can't we all just be Americans?"

Different Identities

Modern American society is absorbed in the interests and passions of the few and their faction. This type of absorption has been part of our nation's history from the beginning. Each of the groups that garner much of the media attention amount to about 1 percent or less of the overall population,[1] which now exceeds 320 million. Media attention often infuses concerns by repeated exposure, magnifying the issues to larger-than-life status. As a result, smaller groups are thrust forward into culture by the attention given. The use of modern technology assists in getting out the message to online newsfeeds of the younger generations. Depending on the politics involved, fringe issues become the causes célèbres endorsed by legislators promising special protections and the elites of society lifting up the issues.

Actions like these have certainly made educators' jobs much more difficult. Controversial words and actions have implications and they always play out in America's schools and ultimately challenge families and their values.

The Culture Has Changed

Anecdotes abound in which children are excoriated and shamed at school because they make a comment or ask a question that is disallowed under the current political climate. Gen Z students feel strongly about their views, and students in this generation feel slighted and offended when they are not allowed to question viewpoints of their friends and fellow students. Teachers should remember that students are both a reflection of their parents' viewpoints and that they are in the process of developing their own. If students feel strongly and differently about something that runs counter to the political correctness of the day, they are called out on it. Some argue that this amounts to a reverse form of bullying students into compliance because of a refusal to comply with the new politically correct landscape of the past decade.[2] If so, then this is another example of the cultural marginalization in which Gen Z finds itself.

Teachers are walking such a fine line these days. But even in walking these fine lines, the problem in walking them might unintentionally offend someone. For example, in Charlotte, North Carolina, teachers are told not to refer to their students as boys or girls anymore due to a small percentage of students wrestling with gender confusion or dysphoria.[3]

Gen Z is the newest target of social change. Recent polls indicate that in a poll of about 1,200 registered voters, between 50 and 60 percent favored same-sex marriage.[4] Like abortion, the issues of same-sex marriage or transgender students using the restrooms of their choice show the marginalized nature of Americans. Americans are interesting people. Their views reflect one perspective, but their NIMBY (Not in My Backyard) philosophy demonstrates a disconnection between perspective and pragmatism once an issue is personalized.

The Word Police

The term "word police" connotes some entity keeping an eye on what is said in public and on the Internet. It also pertains today to things said in private. Computer hackers are keeping watch on what Americans discuss in private communications. However, there are chary eyes cast at those seeking to modify the language of others, particularly if their intentions are to "catch and punish" those whose language is deemed impermissible, intolerant, or offensive. Educators must exercise caution with Gen Z because of the extent of the depth of their feelings about social issues. Students are quick to express their opinions all over the Internet. Schools must take care not to sequester one group's dissenting speech while celebrating another group's less acerbic speech. Gen Z is quick to flag unfairness and broadcast its disagreement.

Hypocrisy Sings Loudly

Word police are granted freer reins to refer to *members within a group* by affectionate terms. They are granted cultural immunity. Those same terms used by members *outside a group* are not afforded the same immunity. An examination of popular music genres yields pejoratives, misogyny, racial epithets, and profanities that encroach on most every line of various songs' lyrics. However, anyone singing these songs in the presence of another person or with a group might be seen as a hater.

Hypocrisy exists when the group that most identifies with the genre uses the terms within the lyrics, but others are not permitted the same luxury. Such identities are marked as culture for one group, but as haters and phobic for another. Gen Z is such a sensitive generation, yet many sing and enjoy the music as if there is nothing offensive within it. Are their sensitivities only one-dimensional?

Today some people lose employment and are punished in culture for saying one "off-limits" word deemed culturally insensitive by the word police. Yet those within certain groups can use the terms with impunity. Teachers are challenged today in dealing with Gen Z students who do not know what to say or do with such inconsistencies.

Off-Limits Words

The word police are responsible in the media and politics for assigning shame to anyone who uses a term deemed harmful, offensive, or defamatory. This is a type of *totalitarianism* that upsets many Americans. The presidential election of 2016 made for interesting debates with high school seniors taking United States government and politics classes. For example, on a personal note, very perceptive Gen Z students were emotionally upset and regularly flagged the major news media as unfair for justifying the language of one political party but downplaying the language of another party. Students even brought in online articles and newspaper clippings from various sources to illustrate their points on both sides.

Another good example of the word police is illustrated in the writing and publications of GLAAD (formerly known as Gay & Lesbian Alliance against Defamation), which claims it is proud that it "rewrites the script for LGBTQ acceptance. As a dynamic media force, GLAAD tackles tough issues to shape the narrative and provoke dialogue that leads to cultural change."[5] Part of this effort, among others, is for schools and the media to end the uses of the terms *homosexual, sexual preferences*, or *abnormal*—all of which the group deems defamatory and offensive.[6]

It is imperative that in today's schools teachers guard against supporting one group over another, despite personal positions, cultural popularity, or political sentiments. One would argue that teachers are supposed to live their identities clearly so as to relay the message that identity is important. The question then should be whether teachers are free to share their personal, moral, or religious identities with their classes. In terms of sexuality, the Gay, Lesbian, and Straight Education Network (GLSEN) has made its goal to inform educators of the "need to integrate LGBT issues throughout the curriculum—not just in classes such as health education, but in disciplines such as English, History, Art and Science."[7] Are teachers of Gen Z students now supposed to use the hyphenation straight, gay, lesbian, bisexual, or trans- to prefix all figures in American history?

Some states are following this path. For example, in the case of California, the new social studies curriculum frameworks emphasize gay and lesbian contributions to American history. In Illinois, Chicago public schools will begin addressing gay lifestyles in kindergarten. Other states and cities are also moving in these directions. We are now straining out so much of our identities and there will soon be very little left in the colander of Americanism.

The identity movement has flourished under former president Obama. Obama has been the highest-profile social justice advocate since the Civil Rights era of the 1960s. There is great irony in this. The former president whose American birth citizenship had been challenged by Donald Trump and fringe conspiracy groups turned out to be one of the most ardent defenders of the identity movement,[8] while the challenger became the nation's forty-fifth president. Many Gen Z students only know the administration of President Obama. Things will change for those younger Gen Z students coming through America's public schools.

FEELINGS ARE THE NEW IDENTITY

Lessons, projects, and technology focusing down on social and emotional learning are elevating students' feelings to levels once reserved for cognition and thought. Welcome to the new identity. What students think about themselves is not so much who they are any longer. Thoughts can be tricky when expressed, but today in classrooms all across America feelings are becoming the new absolutes. Rather than ask questions about student thoughts, encouraging critical analysis and application of certain literary principles, many teachers now ask questions such as, "How did you feel when you read the story?" Opinions based on feelings are fast becoming the norm.

What students are today is what they feel they are. This is subjective reality and this reality is now recognized as truth. Older generations are not so quick to cast aside cognition for emotions in favor of the realizations of a newer generation. Some veteran teachers trained decades ago again view this current trend with a bit of humor. A recent *Babylon Bee* satirical piece illustrates this humor.

One example of a problem given to illustrate the updated standards asked students to figure out when a 6:00 a.m. train leaving Boston at thirty miles per hour and a 7:00 a.m. Milwaukee train headed the opposite direction at forty miles per hour will intersect. A list of possible solutions to the sample problem published in the Common Core standards obtained by reporters indicated that "Ugh," "I'm offended," "Triggered," "Trains scare me," "Boston scares me," "Milwaukee scares me," and "Kill yourself," would all be scored as correct.

"Any emotion, feeling, statement, or catchphrase is an acceptable answer to most of the problems in the new mathematics standards," a Common Core representative told reporters. "As long as students are being sincere, genuine, authentic, and true to themselves at the time they are answering the question, that's all we can ask as educators."

"Who are we to tell anyone that their own mathematical truth is wrong?" the rep added. According to the rep, the Common Core standards will be updated next year to include feelings as acceptable responses to any and all questions pertaining to biology, chemistry, grammar, and history, while sources claim that English literature teachers have already been accepting emotions as responses for years.[9]

Contrast the satirical piece with the following anecdote. A high school senior complained to the teacher after feeling belittled during an important classroom discussion. The complaint by the student was based on "feeling" discomfort, which resulted from a comment made by a fellow student. The student accused of causing the discomfort was bringing up things that were read about law enforcement policies surrounding the constitutionality of a police tactic known as "stop and frisk." The student asked why it was practiced and whether it reduced crime in New York City under then mayor Rudy Giuliani. The student claiming discomfort has been warned by other teachers to watch out for trigger words and to report the incidents when triggers were not used.

At the end of a class session, the eighteen-year-old offended student's emotions were said to have been injured after overhearing a classmate's reference to a certain part of New York City as a "ghetto." It turned out that the student was quoting a policeman from an article that was read on the subject. The student felt belittled merely by the use of the term and the proximity of the student making the comment. The complaint was that a classmate looked in her direction when using the term "ghetto."

Even the most innocent of circumstances can be flagged today as inappropriate if a student feels a personal affront. This is an example of emotions becoming reality—and a false reality, besides. However, students are taught that if something makes them feel badly, then the feelings are real, and so is the offense—regardless of the intent of the person who might have been the offender. Teachers of Gen Z students are still working through this new web of social and emotional realities in the classroom.

A Certain Rationale

The reason to bring all of these issues into a discussion regarding Gen Z students and teachers is that state legislatures are passing laws to embed these social changes directly into some of their social studies and literature curricula. Conservative politicians view this as a virus infecting the nation's students.[10] Nevertheless, all teachers have to cope with social change and how it impacts what and how they teach today's Gen Z students in their classes. Hopefully teachers will be able to find ways to navigate the minefield of vehement disagreement between those marginalized and those polarized. If history is any indicator, the nation is on the edge of a culture war over issues facing Gen Z.

Teachers must see to it that these students are protected in their views and not labeled as bigots or bullies because they most often reflect their parents' and family's views. This assurance must cut both ways and dissent must be allowed. Teachers must also see to it that those who are within their rights to claim something about their identity are also not marginalized. Disagreement is good for democracy. Riots, violence, and property destruction are not.

The challenge for teachers today in the era of social and politically protected identities is to walk the tenuous—and often ambiguous—fine line in their classrooms. They can do this by setting aside their personal beliefs and focusing on creating an environment of respect through teaching students the bounty of the First Amendment freedoms and by allowing students to agree to disagree agreeably. In so doing, teachers then support the students, their families, and recognize the winds of change that will affect twenty-first-century American public schools.

EVERYONE GETS A TROPHY AND A FREE LUNCH

American children have been indoctrinated from the playpen with concepts such as sharing, taking turns, and being kind to one another. Politicians have enacted legislation to guarantee economic and political fairness as a means to level certain economic outcomes for groups. As children they begin to play sports, join clubs, learn that winning isn't everything, and that everyone should learn to carry their own loads. Today, inserted into the minds and hearts of American children is a belief they come in contact with almost every day. That belief is that everyone should be guaranteed to have the same outcomes in life.

Imagine a child on a mathematics team without an excellent grasp on mathematics thinking or in a spelling bee with spelling skills outside the repertoire necessary at certain age. Participation and failure are good things on some levels. However, in today's America, schools, families, and communities at large seem to believe that mere participation is equivalent to all-out effort. There is the expectation that honors, awards, certificates, and trophies will be given to them for "being there" out of a sense of fairness of presence and justice.

Gen Z suffers from a mindset that has settled into its psyche. This mindset is that life is fair and that government, which includes schools, must see to it that everyone has the same conditions in which they live—except for those at the top calling the shots for the rest. The problem with a government like this is the application of any sort of fairness stemming from those whose living conditions emulate gradations of social and economic unfairness. Things were different in previous generations, as illustrated in table 4.1.

Concepts of the American Dream

The American Dream has always been assumed between two basic concepts. The first concept is that people have an opportunity to make a better life for themselves and their families. The second concept is that people should not expect government to give them things just because someone else has them.[11]

The two concepts of opportunity and outcome comprise the axiom that Americans have the opportunity to succeed, but not the guarantee of the outcome or condition possessed by others.[12] Certainly, Americans are compassionate people. But what should be done to balance this compassion with the current expectation of Gen Z in terms of entitlement?

Table 4.1. Comparison of five American generations

Category	Gen Z	Gen Y Millennials	Gen X	Baby Boomers	Traditionalists
Estimated Range of Birth Years Assigned	1995–2010+ Shares Broad Estimate Years	Broad 1981–2005 Narrow 1981–1994	1965–1980	1946–1964	1925–1945
Nicknames	Entitled Generation; Net Geners; iGen	"Me, Me" Generation	Me Generation		Silent Generation; Traditional Generation; Greatest Generation
Presidential Administrations	Clinton; Bush 43; Obama; Trump	Reagan; Bush 41; Clinton; Bush 43	Johnson; Nixon; Ford; Carter	Truman; Eisenhower; Kennedy; Johnson	Coolidge; Hoover; FDR; Truman
Key Value	Purpose	Realistic	Skepticism	Optimism	Loyalty
Characteristics	Personal Entitlement; Work by Choice; Environment Concerns	Personal Safety; Digital and Cyber Literacy	Lack of Trust in Institutions; Adaptive to Technology; Self-Reliant	Questioning of Authority and Institutions; Skeptical	Faith Work; Not Wasting Anything
Historical Events That Influenced	Similar to Millennials; Digital Natives; Diversity; Marriage Redefinition; Progressive Politics; Social Paradigm Changes	Explosion in Tech Growth; Digital Natives; Progressive Politics; Diversity; Crimes and Gangs; Political Correctness	Television; Handheld Games; Personal Computer; Divorce Rate	Suburban Life; Television; Vietnam; Rock and Roll; Drug Culture	WWI; Roaring 20s; Great Depression; WWII, Korean War

	Millennials; Socially Conscious; Socially Active	Literacy; Global Concerns	Technology	Challenge; Competitive	Legacy; Common Sense
Goals in Life	Find Purpose; Work Smarter; Financial Success	Building Several Careers	Building Careers That Are Portable	Building a Career	Leaving a Legacy
View of Institutions	Work for Companies; Work Independently	Each Person Judged by His or Her Work	Doubt of Institutions	Work for Change	Pledge Loyalty
Career Path	Several Paths to Success; Entrepreneurship	Several Paths to Success	Changing Jobs Is a Necessity	Stay at One Job and Build	Stay at One Job
Technology	Radio; Telephone; Television; Personal Computer; Internet; Digital Smart Devices; Wi-Fi	Radio; Telephone; Television; Personal Computer; Internet; Digital Smart Devices; Wi-Fi	Radio; Telephone; Television; Personal Computer; Internet	Radio; Telephone; Television; Computer	Radio; Telephone; Television
Highest Levels of Education	College; Graduate School; Trades; Technology; Entrepreneurs	College; Graduate School; Trades; Technology	College; Graduate School; Trades	High School; College; Trades	High School; Trades
Incentives	Setting of Schedule; Work-at-Will; Entrepreneurship	Meaningful Work; Purposeful Work	Work to Attain Desired Lifestyle	Recognition; Title; Money	Intrinsic Motivation; Personal Satisfaction

| Preferred Available Mode of Communication | Social Media; Smartphone Videos; Twitter; Instagram; Snapchat; Texting | E-mail, Texting; Social Media; Cell Phones; File Sharing | Face-to-Face; Telephone; Cell Phone; E-mail; Instant Messaging | Face-to-Face; Telephone | Face-to-Face; Telephone |

NOT EVERYONE IS PROTECTED

The practice of identity politics today means protection from being offended. There is more attention paid to factional complaints of free speech restriction that might result in a lawsuit than there seems to be paid on behalf of the right of free speech for all. Gen Z is growing up in a culture in which free speech has moved off-center to marginalize protected speech.

Gen Z's speech is being consciously wrought by culture shapers, while at the same time limited by speech police.[13] It all depends which group is exercising their right. In this new America of "my side is right and your side is hateful," there are proactive speech protectionists objectifying expressive free speech while dismissing the speech of others in the process. The proactive protectionists have legislation on their side to ensure punishment for some of the old ways of speaking out.

Getting Their Way

Students of Gen Z are treated delicately across the swath of grade levels in American education. This treatment is found in both public and private schools. For example, whether public or private, there is nothing new about wanting to select the best classes and better teachers for one's children. There is also heavy involvement of parents in private education. This is written about in the first book in this series, *Helping Parents Understand the Minds and Hearts of Generation Z*.

Tactics

The idea that Gen Z is used to finding ways to achieve its desires is more than a generational stereotype. In the minds of Gen Z students, there is a greater willingness to compromise ethics and honesty to achieve desires. For example, in middle and high schools, students are placed into different classrooms after they "try out" their schedules. In these try-outs, they aim to find out what they do not like about a teacher, the work load, the room decorations, the teacher's personality, or whether the class is full of friends. This is the period of exploration before the subsequent academic schedule manipulation.

Students want education their way, which is typical of Gen Z. If their desires are not affirmed, some students then resort to extreme measures. Parents phone the school or district office demanding their child exit one class and be placed in another. It is not uncommon for Gen Z to cry in their counselor's office about their terrible disappointment should their request be declined. Their emotions are so deeply connected to their reality that they cannot accept any other pathway to success aside from their own desires.

Once rejected, Gen Z students' feelings may be so deeply affected that they cannot attend classes for the rest of the school day. Remember, these are the students who later require safe spaces and demand restrictions be placed on groups and individuals. These are the same individuals who selectively deem other groups a risk to their well-being out of fear of microaggression, something factually provocative and disagreeable or even offensive.[14]

Whether at high school or college, Gen Z has an ever-growing reputation of not settling for anything outside their desires. This persistence can be a good trait to have and can lead to other aspects of character development. However, doing whatever is necessary to get what is desired often comes with behaviors that cross the line.

Fabrications

Some of the actions that demonstrate crossing the line are found when students make up stories to force the hands of their counselors to make changes to their class schedules. Fabrication of outright lies over life concerns and emergencies at home has found its way into the laps of decision makers. Begging parents is also a tactic used by Gen Z. Soon enough, parents phone principals to discuss matters concerning their children. There is little left to imagine why Gen Z students are uncompromising.[15] Victories like these for students add to their moral victory trophy case.

These are just samples of how students have learned to get their way. Some of the many elementary principals in this author's sphere shared stories about helicopter and bulldozer parents using similar tactics to affect their child's placement in one classroom or another.[16] Whether secondary or elementary and middle school, the consensus is that people simply do what it takes to win, and this includes parents and students.[17]

Applying Pressure

All teachers of honors and advanced placement classes—and even dual-enrollment college credit classes—often apply a strict and arduous placement process. Staff meetings often occur to discuss each student who has applied for a seat in any of these classes. Once the application process is exhausted and all students have been considered, the class lists are set. Most policies allow students to change classes within a window of time before settling into their schedule and routine. This means that after the routine is established, students are usually not allowed to change schedules. However, after the routines are established, three things usually occur, and often against teachers' wishes.

First, those students originally not placed in the classes of their choice begin to pressure adults with the ability to change their schedules. Friends recruit other friends. Parents communicate with other parents. Social media is lit up. Counselors are told of teenagers crying at home and soon afterward the once-set policy makes exceptions. Parents' complaints to fearful counselors and administrators work their magic and suddenly a student who did not qualify for a challenging program of classes is placed into one or more of these classes. The word "no" has become a starting point for "yes" in far too many counselors' and administrators' offices.

Second, counselors sometimes just place "grieving" students in classes without consultation. Teachers are then surprised when they come to realize that no one recommended these placed students and that the students did not apply prior to the deadline. Teachers then "feel" disrespected and wonder why there is even an application or selection process at all.

Third, students decide that they want an easier schedule, so they put up a series of arguments as to why they do not want to take the classes for which they applied and were placed.

The fact is that in today's schools in America, Gen Z students and parents almost always get their way with counselors and administrators. The newer teachers coming into the profession from Gen Z will have to face the onslaught of pressure that once favored them as students. It will be interesting to see how they hold up against the pressure.

STUDENT-CENTERED SCHOOLS

One of the examples of the expectations of Gen Z students is the presumption that teachers will acquiesce to students' wishes because everyone understands that schools are student-centered. As the philosophy states, *if students wish to turn in homework late or not at all, teachers should just understand that is the way things are today.* Holding students accountable is less acceptable today. This reality marks a very real difference across generations, when students were considered somewhat more responsible and parents supported schools and teachers, sometimes to the detriment of their children. Today the assumption is that parents accept the word of their children more often than they accept the word of the teacher.

In a student-centered school, teachers have given scores to students only to inflate them so that they can compete on after-school extracurricular sports teams. Students failing required classes are pulled from classes and provisions are made to enroll them in online courses where sometimes the parents do the work for their children from home. All of this just so they can remain eligible for sports and then graduate. Truthfully, if every Gen Z student receives a diploma, what did they earn beside another certificate with several names on it?

A RUDE AWAKENING: GEN Z IN THE MARKETPLACE

Barbara Kahn, marketing professor and director of the Jay H. Baker Retailing Center at the Wharton School of Business (UPenn), writes: "The biggest financial event of Gen Z's lifetime is the Great Recession . . . widely considered the worst global downturn since World War II."[18] Dan Schawbel, author of *Promote Yourself*, adds that members of Gen Z are more likely to practice fiscal restraint and demonstrate conservative financial practice compared to their Gen Y counterparts.[19] He also writes, "They've seen millennials suffer under the weight of student loans; they've seen them be underemployed and they've witnessed their delayed adulthood . . . members of Gen Z don't want that."[20] Gen Z teenagers are especially more frugal about finances than those before them.[21]

Previous generations refer to this newest generation by the phrase "Gen Y on steroids."[22] There is truth in the statement the "children of Gen X, they don't know what life is like without the Internet. Twenty-three million strong and growing. . . . Gen Z also has a bit of ego—at least in the eyes of the other generations—and they're used to putting their whole lives online, telling their friends and anyone else who will listen everything they're doing, from brushing their teeth to sitting in traffic to getting a promotion. . . . Gen Z is definitely one to watch. Before you know it, they're going to be in the workplace gunning for your job."[23] But they will have to enter the workplace with a set package of skills requisite for success, according to Rachel Gillett.

As a former Harvard admissions interviewer, she has observed that there are four very important skills all students need to have as part of their skill set by age eighteen.[24] These skills are prerequisites to success in college and beyond and include 1) the ability to manage money and finances, 2) the growing responsibility to manage time, 3) the skills to manage and resolve conflict that arises, and 4) the developing ability to maintain a positive attitude and disposition in the face of adversity.[25] There is nothing in the list about safe spaces, avoiding conflict, emoting to manipulate others in order to get one's way, or play out one's reality through feelings.

GEN Z AND ECONOMICS

A recent online TD Ameritrade Investor Index survey of Gen Z students (n=1,001) and Gen Z parents (n=1,000) provides insights into the economic expectations of both. The survey was sent out across the United States, with each of the reporting geographical region's respondents equally divided between male and female.[26] The results have serious implications for the future of America.

Accuracy of Work. It is clear from the survey that Gen Z considers themselves as focusing on accuracy of work more than they focus on the speed at which work is accomplished. This is interesting in that Gen Z uses technology for speed. This Gen Z student viewpoint pertaining to work affects their views about life, as well as their perception about their own personality traits such as being ambitious, flexible, and accepting.[27]

Economic Concerns. Throughout the survey, those on the upper edge of Gen Z, the college-age group, showed slight dissimilarities to their parents' views on today's economic questions. Here are a few examples. The parents of Gen Z students responded that their biggest economic worries were about jobs and unemployment (25 percent). Gen Z students responded with the same issue as their highest worry (26 percent).[28]

The parents viewed not having enough money as a concern (10 percent), and their children placed this same concern at 8 percent. One additional issue considered was the national debt. Parents viewed this issue at 6 percent, while the children placed it at 5 percent in terms of their concern economically. On several other issues, the parents and their Gen Z children were between 1 and 3 percent apart.[29]

Top Three Overall Concerns. The top three concerns that Gen Z students expect to encounter in their lives are 1) having personal identity stolen (40 percent), 2) affording college (39 percent), and 3) large student loan balance (39 percent). Again, these are not dissimilar to the parents surveyed, where two of the top three concerns were nearly identical. Parents stated their top three concerns as 1) affording college (42 percent), 2) not concerned about anything (37 percent), and 3) large student loan balance (36 percent).[30] These concerns reflect what researchers already have discovered about children and their parents. The former reflect the latter on many issues.

Finances. The majority of Gen Z students did not have any significant savings plans or checking accounts (55 percent). This was not the case with their parents, where 56 percent had at least a savings plan and a checking account (40 percent). "Not surprisingly, older age groups are significantly more likely to have financial products than younger groups."[31] Given that a good number of Gen Z is now in its twenties, its financial practices may change as it continues to age.

Expectations. Gen Z has very lofty expectations for careers, often stating they want companies to pursue them and pay them a very nice salary. They feel entitled to call their own shots in the marketplace, often thinking much more of themselves than what is pragmatic. Furthermore, Gen Z expects employers to grant them time to pursue causes and leave their generational mark and legacy on culture. Gen Z has shown its propensity to demonstrate very little allegiance to things beyond their interests.

That being said, the expressions of Gen Z's interests are quite fickle and are as reliable as their loyalty to work they do not enjoy. If they do not perceive they are making a difference socially, they will choose another form of employment that values their positions. In typical Gen Z fashion, they feel the economy revolves around them. Contrast Ameritrade's survey with a summary of an informal national survey conducted by this author that appears in the conclusion of this chapter.

THE FUZZY FUTURE OF GEN Z

Some people view Gen Z through skeptical eyes. Adults are often taken aback by some outlandish ideas and assumptions of the generations that come after them. Generally, Baby Boomers, Gen Xers, and Millennials frown at some of the statements made by the newest generation in terms of their economic and personal expectations. An examination of these expectations offers little difficulty toward understanding why so many of Gen Z are quick to gripe and complain when they do not get what they want. However, Gen Z is only half of the story.

Parents of Gen Z should not be surprised by what they have created. The following list illustrates some of the reasons why Gen Z has inordinate expectations. The following comments were given to teachers and illustrate the future of Gen Z students through the words of their parents.[32]

- "The drinks in the cafeteria aren't cold enough."
- "He doesn't respect you because you're shorter than him."
- "Please don't contact me about my daughter's behavior."
- "I don't do homework, so why should my son?"
- "Can you stop asking her to put up her hand before talking? It isn't very encouraging of her ideas."
- "He's only bullying people because he's more developed than them."
- "Please don't correct her spelling; it knocks her confidence."
- "Can you call me if you see her hanging out with the boys?"
- "Our family policy is to have our children *only* do homework that matches our parenting philosophy."
- "I don't know where you went to school, but in the Ivy League . . ."
- "He doesn't do this at home."
- "My daughter needs an older teacher."
- "I'm so sorry to interrupt while you're having dinner out with your wife, but if you could just give me a quick summary of how my son is doing in your class, that would be great."
- "I'd like to observe your teaching style, but I don't want to make you nervous. Is it OK if I just stand in the doorway for a while each morning?"
- "I know my daughter has a little fever today, but it's only allergies."
- "Our family believes in freedom of speech, so we don't limit our child's vocabulary. So if Bonnie swears in class, understand that we expect you not to call attention to it."
- "What did you do to provoke him to bite?"
- "It's your job to make sure he doesn't use slang."
- "All the teachers from his previous school and now all the teachers at your school are complaining about his behavior. You're all picking on him."
- "My child would never lie."
- "How do I get him to stop watching so much porn?"
- "I don't understand why he's acting up in school. He's got the house to himself."
- "We showed a mother CCTV footage of her son stealing a teacher's wallet. The mother said we had 'used our digital editing department to superimpose her son's head onto another student's body.' We didn't even have a library, let alone a digital editing department."

- "I had a parent teacher conference for a student that was acting out. Parents were not together and *despised* each other. Dad made it a top priority to come early and let me know that his child was a one-night-stand baby, that mom was a drug addict, and that he conceived a child with the devil."
- "Said they thought I faked my chemistry degree. Admins did not support me either. Ended up having to take a somewhat informal test administered by a doctor who was another one of my students' parents to prove I had actually studied chemistry."
- "This year, I was asked if I work in special education because I couldn't get a job teaching 'regular kids.'"
- "She doesn't have a bedtime. . . . Of course if she is tired in the morning, I don't force her to go to school."
- "A mom made us stop playing Disney music because 'it was bad for her daughter's self-esteem.'"
- "I am a racist because I did not give her child an A on a paper she chose to write on President Obama. The fact that it was poorly written, unsupported by factual evidence, and completely disorganized apparently should not be taken into consideration."
- "My son is struggling so much. Can you send home a copy of the test ahead of time so he can prepare?"
- "Science is hurting my child."
- "His father called and complained to the vice principal that I had been too hard on his son and was 'trying to fill his head with ideas.'"
- "A parent once excused her child's stealing by claiming it was a result of his diabetes."
- "My daughter can't do that because her brain is shrinking. The doctor said so."

Some parents are teaching their children exactly what is fast emerging as the Gen Z stereotype. Students are taught how to act when they want something and will not settle for other than what they desire. Children are also taught how to work around the problem to get what they seek, whether they earn it or not. Future employers are not going to hire workers like this. But if they do, they won't be on the job for long. Unless the trajectory changes for Gen Z, they are headed for serious concerns once they graduate from high school or college and head off into the workforce in the coming years.

CONCLUSION: GEN Z'S FEELINGS ON ISSUES

Four hundred sixty-two (n=462) Gen Z students from ages fourteen to twenty-two were surveyed recently. Colleagues and homeschool parents from around the nation shared a Survey Monkey link with students and assisted in the distribution of the survey. The students were asked to respond to a series of ten questions and three of the questions and responses are presented below for teachers to appreciate. They also serve as the conclusion to this chapter and should receive serious consideration by teachers of the current generation.

Digital Literacy

Digital literacy was broken into three categories. First, 82.5 percent of the respondents claimed to be *digital natives*, which means they claim to understand digital technology and have been familiar with computers, smartphones, and the Internet from an early age. Second, 16 percent of the respondents claimed to be *digital immigrants*. A digital immigrant is a person who has become familiar with computers, smartphones, and the Internet within the last one to three years. The last category for student responses was *digital foreigner* Only seven out of 462 students (1.5 percent) responded that they know what smart technology is and that they even have a smartphone, but they are not well versed in how to use them.

Things That Frustrate Gen Z

The following statements are free responses given anonymously and without regard to age or gender. Three hundred and two (n=302) statements were included as responses to this question. Some of the more interesting and poignant responses are listed below, and these responses run the gamut.

- They passed along their debt to us.
- Millennials are allowing socialism.
- Baby Boomers ruined our economy and now I am in debt for the rest of my life.
- Gen Xers do not understand us.
- Other generations think they know everything.
- Often they tease our generation for having our noses in our screens, but I see other generations doing it and nothing is said.

- The 1990s were better than now because we had more face-to-face interaction.
- Boomers are hyperjudgmental, especially of our work ethic.
- They expect us to adopt their ways of living and call us lazy for not doing so.
- They talk about how difficult their lives were when in reality we have different problems.
- They do not understand the competitiveness when applying to college.
- Previous generations treat us like children and then expect us to act like adults.
- They think all teenagers are the same in every generation.
- I get annoyed when I have to help my parents to use their smartphones.
- Those other generations do not like change.
- The previous generations were the ones with all the talent and we are left with the scraps.
- Baby Boomers are very strict.
- Millennials are very clique-oriented and do not make room for us.
- Economics have changed since the 1970s and people need to understand this.
- I am kind of envious that previous generations were able to afford things at earlier ages.
- Millennials think they are always right.
- They cannot relate to a lot of modern issues regarding social and technological issues.

Suggestions to Make Education Better

Included below is a list of several of Gen Z students' suggestions in terms of making education better for them.

- More scholarships to make college more affordable.
- Include classes in high school that are based on students' dream jobs.
- More options for career paths.
- Changing the curriculum to things that are more important to our futures.
- Teach material that we will actually use when we are adults.
- Math could use a shot in the arm that is not Common Core.
- Find teachers that actually care more about students.
- Stop worrying about wrong things like dress codes.
- Stop the labeling of groups.

- Use modern technology to learn rather than forcing us to put away the technology that we have become accustomed to using.
- We know you are the ones with the degrees and such and know how to teach. But we are the ones who know how to connect and make the process of education go as smoothly as possible.
- Take away our phones. Make us read something for once. Make it mandatory to take a "preparation for life" class.
- Not so much cell phone use in class. More one on one with teachers.
- Lower tuition.
- Reform the K–12 education system in America.
- Better teachers in poverty-stricken areas.
- Don't forget about the higher-achieving students.
- Have a class specifically for explaining some things that come with adult life.

The future for Gen Z can be as bright as they want it to be. There is more than enough room across generations to share in American culture and in the American economy. Gen Z has to learn to put down its devices and look up. In so doing, they will capture the image that many educators already perceive. That is, the horizon is clear and bright and one does not have to Google that to experience it.

Chapter Five

Success with Gen Z

Teaching students how to balance technology usage along with offline socializing and interpersonal skills is essential. But it is irresponsible to proclaim that technology simply distracts, diminishes social skills, and holds lesser value than other content areas. And to do so not only lets our students down, but also negates the mission statements emblazoned on the walls of our schools.[1]

Chapter 5 includes the following ten major sections: 1) understanding how Gen Z learns, 2) Gen Z's social media preferences, 3) using smartphones for success with Gen Z, 4) engaging the distracted, 5) classroom management and smartphones, 6) reaching different types of Gen Z students, 7) are teachers prepared to work with Gen Z students? 8) implications for teachers, 9) making a difference by being a different teacher, and 10) conclusion.

Technology is here to stay. Smart devices are permanent fixtures in American education. Educational technology is making deep imprints on student learning and has embedded itself in American culture. Teachers already enrolled in teacher training are practicing learning strategies using technology that might be outdated by the time they graduate.

Technology is changing the ways education is delivered and soon newer teachers will be completely surrounded by educational technology in the classroom. One thing is certain as it pertains to Gen Z: schools and teachers who hope to realize success with this emerging generation must become immersed in their world of smart technology.

UNDERSTANDING HOW GEN Z LEARNS

Depending on the grade levels taught, the type of work, and amount of technology involved in classrooms, instruction and learning will vary. Teacher success today is measured all too often only by education professionals and not by other teachers. Student success is also measured today by parents' expectations of student happiness and well-being. For better or for worse, these rank highly in the minds of Gen Z parents. Gen Z students' senses of belonging and social and emotional wellness are definite competitors with academic progress and well-being.

Gen Z students' learning is measured more and more by a variety of inquiry-based and project-based tasks. These tasks are associated with the utilization of technology in student work production, which also includes the ability of students to have fun while learning. Students learn to communicate their ideas effectively and cogently—all of which makes students happy people.

Technology and Student Interactions

For example, a second-grade class might be using technology in more sensory ways than students in middle schools or junior highs. High school students might be designing robots, coding applications, working on seamless programming, or even taking aviation courses. If schools and teachers are not incorporating some forms of technology within their classrooms on a regular basis, classroom management may well become problematic. Students' abilities to interact while engaged in their work are most critical.

We have arrived at the age in which technology not only serves as a learning tool, but it also serves as a tool for classroom management and discipline. Student attention spans and smartphone addictions are joint problems that do not diminish because a student sits in a classroom five days a week. Students do not become less distracted because a teacher places piles of worksheets in front of them. Again, depending on the classroom, the grade levels, and the ages of the students, technology can be used differently to move toward maximizing learning, best approached in stages throughout the school day.

Personal anecdotes abound in which students demonstrate a lack of self-control and are even completely out of control in classrooms. Some of these students have biological or neurological issues, such as ADHD or chemical imbalances, including those diagnosed as bipolar. Certainly there are students mixed in who are otherwise normal acting and energetic children in America's public schools. All of these students seem to have one great thing in common. They are calmed and on task for a time, especially while earphones are squeezed onto their heads or while ear buds are plugged into their ears.

The old adage that "music soothes the savage beast" can be updated to include modern technology's sights and sounds. Today's technology can soothe the hyperactive and distracted. However, teachers should not be fooled by this. All technology accomplishes at junctures such as these is to provide many sensory distractions over and against the student's package of latent distractions. That being said, teachers are amazed at how even their worst-behaving students shape up if they are learning at play while using some form of technology. The tools used correctly are really quite amazing. Most students today do not have the academic acumen or attention spans to listen to another person talk or follow directions without finding something else interrupting their lines of thinking.

The truth bears repeating time and time again. The brains of students today are wired very differently. Teachers from older generations may choose to battle this reality and in some cases find victory. Newer teachers replacing those of previous generations may choose to utilize the current technologies, which may bypass their comfort levels of utility, just to engage students and work within the parameters of their current Gen Z students' wiring and learning propensities. Learning more about Gen Z students cannot help but produce more effectiveness as a teacher. Greater effectiveness with students has the capacity to improve learning outcomes. That is a win-win situation.

GEN Z'S SOCIAL MEDIA PREFERENCES

The consideration of Gen Z's preferences of communication is like asking what a teenager is in the mood to eat for lunch on any given day. Variations and impulses change like the direction of the wind. There is some great information that can be gleaned from surveys of Gen Z. For example, there is a certain reliability in examining collected lists from social media sites. The Fluent Group performed a recent survey of students ages seventeen to twenty-four from March 1 to 4, 2016.[2] The survey was interested in determining strategies of marketing college and wanted to see where those mostly from

Gen Z "hung out" online. The sample was significant (1,310 college students) and the findings were quite interesting.

Facebook is still the most significantly used platform for social media among the group (67 percent), followed by Snapchat (51 percent) and then by Instagram (50 percent). Among the Snapchat users, those students stated it was used primarily for communicating with friends while at school.[3]

The implications for teachers are interesting and challenging. Reaching students who spend four to six hours each day posting, checking, and responding to various online forums can be challenging—especially from the context of what teachers had always thought was "protected time" in the classroom. The question remains, how should teachers use Gen Z students' customary and natural inclinations for communication to their advantage in teaching and learning?

One thing is definite. If teachers flip the classroom to some degree—and this includes college classrooms—and record things for students to watch online, they will partake. Nearly 53 percent of the students said that YouTube is their platform of choice for following celebrities and those with millions of subscribers.[4] If teachers plan on reaching Gen Z from where they are, then they have to show up in online places they call home. Gen Z is definitely visual and emotional in their makeup, preferring images and videos to texting and e-mail.[5]

However, teachers must be wary and cautious when it comes to what and where they post comments. Not too long ago, the teacher's lounge was the place of venting and over the line comments about students, parents, fellow teachers, and administrators. Today, with the ease of posting on social media and the sense of privacy one feels from home, teachers are involving themselves more and more online. Teachers must take care not to reveal their true feelings to the general public. They must also be very cautious not to post anything impulsive about their students and their parents—even in jest. The bottom line is that teachers should not become too cozy with social media platforms that are shared with students.

The Costs of Coziness

As mentioned in an earlier chapter, several teachers had to resign when it was determined by a hacker that they had posted comments about their students on a site online. Slack is a team-oriented website where professionals and others can collaborate and share via posts, messages, and various other forms of communication.[6] Teachers were outed in what they thought was private conversation online and were forced to resign in disgrace. A hacker posted what the teachers wrote online and then everything fell apart from there. What they posted was politically incorrect as well as technologically incorrect for professionals.[7]

Now what might be deemed in jest for one generation is easily misunderstood by another generation. Seeking a pound of flesh for the perceived offense is sometimes set in motion by the offended. Success with Gen Z students requires that teachers demonstrate consistent behaviors online and in person. While what was posted on Slack might be taken as humorous by many and venting by others, there are people with either different senses of emotional realities, personal vendettas, or whose brains are wired to be easily hurt who must be considered.[8] In this case, the "Slack attack" was initiated by a hacker, then sent around the Rhode Island Charter Prep School via a Google document.[9]

Gutter is as gutter does, in the view of those who study these issues. Teachers have freedom of expression indeed. However, such freedom is not absolute, especially when it comes to students. This is what teachers tell their students every day. This fact is no different from public schools, charter schools, or private schools. The lessons learned can be difficult. Success with Gen Z students does not arrive for teachers becoming like their students. This includes how and when teachers use smartphones in class. With this understanding, are there ways to utilize smartphones for the classroom to the benefit of learning and to harness and maximize some of the power within the tool itself?

USING SMARTPHONES FOR SUCCESS WITH GEN Z

There are hundreds of fun and easy ways for students, teachers, and parents to take advantage of the powerful pocket computer called the smartphone. Smartphone technology comes with cameras, and apps can be downloaded for nearly every learning tool imaginable. There are websites for students on which they can register with their phones and take surveys, review for tests, and do many other things. Smartphones that are available today are Wi-Fi Internet capable, and many schools are wired for access.

The rise of technology brings with it the genius of innovation in terms of ways to utilize the devices. Lisa Kolb suggests the following ways to use smartphones in the classroom and at home: 1) Students can become documentarians, capturing moments on their cameras or recording events; 2)

Children can become better writers, both in the formal sense and with a textual shorthand, which can be used later to expand into something more formal; 3) Students can become quasi-expert historians in subject matter by researching, reading, recording, and thereby analyzing critically what they read and see; and 4) Families can become more organized and assist students with their daily calendaring, demonstrating appropriate ways to utilize social media, continuing to model and remind their children that what is posted on the Internet is always going to be there.[10]

Capturing Moments

Gen Z students are all about instantaneous notoriety and immediate gratification. They would prefer to see themselves and others in Snapchat and compete for attention socially with their friends. If students were shown ways to take advantage of their instant need for gratification and also accumulate a tidy portfolio for the sake of academics, they would then be applying skills simultaneously with their itch to be seen and heard.

Creative teachers must apply their creativity to engage Gen Z students differently today. Veteran teachers could learn much from the newly credentialed teachers who may have come out of high-tech teacher training institutions. Implementing new and exciting ways to use technology in the classroom would not only be fun, but would draw the teacher directly into the wheelhouse of learning with Gen Z students. Teachers of every generation can benefit from opportunities to connect on different levels with their students.

For example, students performing service in the community could record themselves, knowing their recording would then extend into two areas of their lives: one social and one academic. The academic area would require additional editing and would need to meet additional requirements for a grade, while the posting of the raw footage or edited version to their social media accounts would fulfill the desire for instant gratification. Chances are the students would post clips of their service all over the Internet, possibly on their own video channels.

As teacher education institutions continue to deepen their partnerships with local schools, the uses of educational and social technologies will increase. How these will be utilized in the classroom is limited only to individual teachers, school policies, and access to the technology. Given that most students today have smartphones already with them at school, particularly from middle and junior high upward, technology is no longer something each school has to go out and secure. Wi-Fi Internet plans are now more affordable schoolwide and it is feasible for teachers to become tech-savvy in short order. It is time to engage Gen Z squarely in the midst of their reality.

ENGAGING THE DISTRACTED

In some ways, teaching and education have much in common with advertising and branding. Advertisers make every effort to reach and connect with consumers, hoping those consumers will take hold of what is offered. Teaching is a lot like advertising, especially given what is already known of the propensities, habits, compulsions, and traits of Gen Z. Given that there are so many variables of distraction for Gen Z, it is imperative to reach them where they are—right in the middle of their distractions—if regular connections are to occur.

If teachers are going to make these connections, then it requires knowing students well enough and understanding what makes them think and act the ways they do. Classroom teachers are quite savvy and highly intuitive professionals. However, the reader would be advised to revisit chapter 3 of the first book in this series. The chapter was written for parents to understand "What makes Generation Z tick and what makes them ticked." The more teachers know about their students, the deeper the levels of respect and the greater the opportunities for partnerships for learning.

Reaching Gen Z

Bill Alberti suggests six ways for the sales market to reach Gen Z.[11] Professionals in the field of education could learn much from the field of advertising and marketing. Strategies to reach into the minds and hearts of students in the world of advancing technology are most welcome. Filtering Alberti's advertising strategies through the lens of education yields the following.

First, as a teacher, demonstrating to the students' personal authenticity without inhibitions is seen as a plus. Do not be afraid to be genuinely quirky, engaging, and even funny. Gen Z relates well to these characteristics online and in their real world. Students, although living in a fictional world of virtual reality, can still tell the genuine from a phony.

Second, teachers must be caring and passionate about their work. Avoid coming across as doing a job or acting a certain way just for show, money, or any other reason than love of profession. The world of YouTube has provided Gen Z with a model of authenticity, and the viral nature of some followers of channels and personal videos is evidence of their perception of authenticity. Snapchat's immediacy lends itself to authenticity in the minds of Gen Z. Hence its popularity continues unabated.

Third, connecting what is taught to the real world is a major selling point for Gen Z. They are "cause-worthy" and want to make a difference in the world. They are given to group-think and crowd sourcing. So affecting their impulses and wiring toward causes is a plus in the eyes of Gen Z. See the parallel to advertising here?

Fourth, and it should go without saying, teachers must be online and tech-savvy if they intend to maintain an understanding of the connectivity of Gen Z. Detailed participation is neither required nor recommended. Conversely, teachers who view the tech outlets as little more than annoyances and mere distractions are missing out on understanding the technology channels through which Gen Z shapes their reality.

Fifth, when dividing students into collaborative groups, there is a certain psychology present in each classroom in helping them discover what each has in common. For example, it would be helpful for teachers to discover what interests and activities are part of their overall classes' makeups. Allowing students to discover that several of them enjoy soccer, painting, share religious beliefs, or even like the same foods or styles of music is key. Sharing photos is an excellent way to "advertise" student interests. These types of face-to-face discoveries are essential for Gen Z, which finds its affinities online and socializes accordingly.

Sixth and last, Gen Z is highly distracted, and some of this is by their own choosing. "Never has a generation had more opportunities to be distracted, overstimulated and overscheduled than Gen Z."[12] Teachers are learning what advertisers already know. Alter the approaches used to heighten senses and a deal can be closed. Teachers must understand this and, like those with brands to sell in the marketplace, it is very important to break through the distractions of other brands. In essence, teachers are distractors of the distractions, selling their wares in creative ways. Student and teacher transactions are made each day in the classroom, especially by persuasive personalities and titillating technology.

CLASSROOM MANAGEMENT AND SMARTPHONES

Every school that brings itself into the twenty-first century technologically must contend with policies and procedures on using smartphones in the classrooms and on school campuses. Smart policies for smart technology will take some doing on the parts of administrators. Most administrators are enamored with having their schools known as high-tech. But administrators are not the people in the classrooms having to manage students and their access. However, everything from permission slips to what websites should and should not blocked, as well as dealing with students who violate the in-class policies, must be considered within an overall strategy.

Because data plans are moving toward user-friendly pricing, and the plans associated with data use are edging downward toward free and all-inclusive, students accessing websites in class that are in violation of school policies must be addressed. Just as an aside, there will be students using their own data plans outside the school buffers and firewalls. Teachers are going to have to be aware of what is being accessed by their students. Toward this end, proactive classroom management training and understanding of policies must be shared and discussed among faculty and must involve parents within the school community.

Smart technology not only involves Gen Z with smart hardware, but it also requires involvement of parents, faculty, and administrators working together with their *smart-heart-ware* to derive technology policies that encourage understanding and learning for all involved. Managing the classroom begins long before the students pop out their smartphones to connect.

REACHING DIFFERENT TYPES OF GEN Z STUDENTS

Students come in all shapes and sizes and from many backgrounds. There are no two alike. The upshot of this reality is the germaneness of the methods of teaching and reaching Gen Z students in the classroom. Strategies that work one day or even for a mere hour do not necessarily have the same impact if applied routinely.

Teaching students from today's Gen Z requires first reaching them. Reaching students comes with the implicit charge to bring to them something of deep interest. The impetus for the teacher is to make certain that something unconventional occurs within the context of the learning experience. The responsibility is on the teacher to marshal the requisite modern tools to present the content in engaging fashion. Preferably, this unconventionality takes advantage of modern technology.

Students across all generations come with an interest in stories. A master storyteller can massage content and context in such ways that students would tune in both intellectually and emotionally. Stories make learning relevant, personal, and practical. They also humanize the teacher to his or her classes. Some of these stories can be personal, always seeking to bring a moral purpose or lesson to apply to students' lives. Elementary teachers have some of the best ideas on applying this strategy.

Stories can be of others, and students can read about these persons and draw much personal and intellectual application. Storytelling has been lost in the academic shuffle, tossed between Common Core and the ESSA. However, in an age in which technology has taken over much of the attention of Gen Z, the human element persists. It persists sometimes as a novelty, but persists nevertheless.

Another aspect of teaching Gen Z has been pushed aside for the sake of meeting some standard or an eventual high-stakes assessment. This is referred to as exploration of student interests and tying these interests to the content of the classes or material for the lessons. For example, teachers could ask students to select some academic areas they would enjoy interwoven in the required content for classes. Younger students could also be asked, delimited of course to the targeted group of categories preselected by the teacher.

The strategy here is that with a host of things available to students online, they sense that they have a direct relationship with assisting in what is learned and this buy-in is quite significant for Gen Z students. There is no mere coincidence between what students enjoy learning and the transference of these areas to long-term memory.

ARE TEACHERS BEING PREPARED TO WORK WITH GEN Z?

What are colleges of teacher education doing to prepare the future teachers of Gen Z? Colleges are burgeoning with students from Gen Z. How is technology used to acquire new skills and increase effectiveness in instructional teaching methods and student learning? The reports are mixed. Schools of education are questioning the relevance of their programs, connecting prospective teachers and the schools calling for teachers, and often students who are immersed in classroom experiences are receiving their baptism by fire.

Under the Every Student Achieves Act (ESSA), states have much more latitude in training their teachers to meet the needs of the local communities. Hopefully the ESSA brings with it serious investment in educational technology and that strings or unintended consequences do not stall progress. There will be differences in the allocations of funds for elementary schools, junior highs, and high schools. The lion's share of educational technology funding may show up in alternative secondary education and career and technical training programs, as well as at colleges and universities in the STEAM (Science, Technology, Engineering, Arts, and Mathematics) areas of focus.

Leveraging Online Classes for Higher Education

The recent fad of massive open online courses or MOOCs that consist of "a variety of materials, from video lectures and assigned readings to quizzes and interactive user forums for instructors, students, and teaching assistants"[13] has all but run its course. In order to gain and hold interest for Gen Z students and move into the twenty-first century, the next generation of MOOCs will have to undergo some serious adjustment to their format. There MOOCs will become "sensorily immersive, leveraging virtual reality to put students in the world they're studying. Instead of having to memorize facts about the Civil War, for example, a student in a future MOOC will be on the battlefield."[14]

Recent indications were that MOOCs are all but dead in favor of different approaches associated with online learning, which comes by way of the needs and desires of the individual.[15] The good news is that MOOCs are being recalibrated to reach Gen Z. The MOOC options are now global and involve some of the world's best universities and can be part of the online community of learning.

Students can now sit anywhere in the world and have access to college classes in the United Kingdom, Asia, and in North America. In fact, "more than 60 universities across the U.K. and Europe have partnered with Future Learn to deliver their courses, mirroring trends of the growth of these online classes in the U.S."[16] The highly technological generation is getting used to education their way, unlike any time prior in history. Educational technology is opening new worlds for students.

Secondary Schools

Newer "modes of online learning will cater more effectively to Generation Z. . . . The oldest Gen Zers have been forced into an industrial model of school, and we are seeing all these attention problems . . . their brains are wired differently and actually function better with input from a variety of sources."[17] MOOCs and online learning appear to bring the future of education to the present and are in better alignment with the way Gen Z thinks about education.

Those who take a different route to a career outside that of the strict academic pursuit will be better served with advancing career technology training. Although some "vocational training has gotten a bad rap for decades . . . it's on the verge of a major makeover."[18] The new buzz phrase referring to vocational training is now "competency-based education, which focuses on the mastery of work-related skills rather than command of a particular academic discipline."[19] Secondary education students will benefit from CBE.

Investors and economic entrepreneurs "are getting in on the action, too, providing mentorship and funding for young people's promising business ideas. Paypal co-founder and serial entrepreneur Peter Thiel is at the forefront of these educational incubators. . . . In 2010, he created the Thiel Fellowship, awarding $100,000 to 20 people under 20 years old in order to spur them to drop out of college and create their own ventures. The Thiel Foundation then launched Breakout Labs, a grant making program that funds radical and innovative science research."[20] Although unconventional in their approach, Gen Z's entrepreneurial spirit finds offers like Thiel's quite tantalizing.

Gen Z's desires for higher education remain intact. The essence of Gen Z's entrepreneurial spirit and their desire to be trained are captured nicely in the statement that they are willing "to attend traditional college. But it's as much (if not more) for the social benefits and networking connections as it is for the skills. Many know what they want to do and already have the means to do it. I wonder if things will come full circle, and like his great-grandfather, my son will choose and train for his first career by the time he's 16."[21]

Gen Z has come to expect educational choices "their way." They express desire on many surveys for education to fit their desires and insist on a plethora of choices to fulfill their personal goals. Secondary schools are moving toward more online classes, allowing students to finish courses in a matter of days or weeks. The proliferation of technology is mainly the cause for these opportunities.

Dual enrollment (DE) courses are quickly becoming the next thing in high school education, but only for those qualified by grades and academic pursuit goals. Dual enrollment allows high school students who are eligible to take classes in their high schools that provide them earned credit for both high school graduation requirements and for college. The credits appear on both transcripts and are usually taught, supposedly, at the Advanced Placement level of difficulty. Soon, it is predicted, DE classes and programs will be open to many students, possibly resulting in a diminishing of the quality of instruction and learning.

One of the drawbacks of this type of program is that it will grow to the detriment of the Advanced Placement (AP) classes. Which students would stay in an AP class with only the possibility of college credit by earning a score of four or five on an AP Exam? Why would they stay in such a class when they can dual enroll, get college credit and high school credit, while taking yearlong courses?

Dual enrollment courses may phase out several Advanced Placement courses within the next few years. Gen Z students will no longer need them to earn college credit. Logically, why would any student take an AP course and have to pay for and pass a test to access the possibility of college credit? Now all students have to do is to take and earn "C grades" in DE classes to ensure the same credits, all with no additional assessments or payments outside the college financial and academic requirements.

Whatever the situation, colleges training Gen Z teachers must partner with local schools through a variety of direct mentorships, professional development, and technology. In order to teach a DE class, the usual requirement is a Master of Arts degree in a content area. Because Gen Z is much more technologically social and prefers social media to information-only media, it is incumbent on postsecondary institutions to recognize this and train future teachers accordingly.

IMPLICATIONS FOR TEACHERS

The characteristics of Gen Z raise a host of questions for educators being trained by older and much more veteran college faculty. In fact, even Millennials are being nudged out by the rapid acceptance of Gen Z and its desire for attention.[22]

The classroom teacher's authority of previous generations has been diminished by three recent developments. The first is Common Core, in which the teacher became more of a moderator of learning rather than a "sage on the stage." Second, access to knowledge is at the students' fingertips, and the

Internet provides understanding to fit their curiosity. As a result, there is little need for students to query teachers in order to discover knowledge and determine answers to questions. Third, "helicopter parents" have usurped teacher authority and have moved to the next phase of control. They are now acting as "bulldozer parents." Each of these has serious implications for teachers of Gen Z and each is addressed in chapter 1 of the first book in this series.

Relevance of Teacher Training

All of these implications beg the question as to the relevance and quality of the training and mentoring of newer teachers in our teacher-training colleges. Likewise, there must be attention paid to whether these newer teachers are entering American schools at a disadvantage—especially with four areas in minds.

First, there is some question as to the lack of understanding of the differences in brain development of Gen Z students and students of previous generations. Being connected digitally by a variety of devices 24/7 is not deemed healthy by anyone, but it exists. Are teachers examining this phenomenon and being asked to consider the best ways to deal with this in their classrooms?

Second, how should teachers handle the rampant narcissism of today's students in the "everyone receives a trophy" entitlement mentality of Gen Z and their parents? In what ways will teachers be instructed to inform students and parents of shortcomings of children, given how easily people are offended today?

Third, to what extent can teachers practice honesty and empathy with the increasing inability to call out and correct poor behaviors or attitudes—especially without being labeled or categorized in a pejorative? In what ways will graduating Gen Z college students begin to reshape the methods of connecting and communicating students' shortcomings?

Fourth, in what ways can teachers use Gen Z's digital communication prowess to their advantage for learning?[23] Students already think they are at an advantage over adults. What should teachers know about technology that relates to education that considers what Gen Z already knows about social media and research tools?

New Directions

What new directions will schools and teachers take to accommodate Gen Z?[24] In answering this query, teachers and administrators should reevaluate their understanding of what accommodation means in the schools and the classrooms.[25] Teachers must undergo yet another set of changes in order to adjust to the release of the stranglehold of Common Core to accept the looser grip of the ESSA. Any new direction taken by school districts must have a comprehensive plan that unfortunately places the newest generation of students as guinea pigs.[26]

Colleges are making every effort to predict the shape of teacher education for the next decade. They have done so with an influx of the newest generation of students. Generations age and move on into higher education and the workforce. Some of these students will become teachers, making efforts to reach back into their generation to make a difference.[27] Some states are holding firm with training students with Common Core methods. As stated earlier, this may change under the Trump administration.

The political implications are many, and education always seems to be caught in the middle. Based on this reality, the question to explore then is, "What is the future of education with Generation Z,"[28] given the fuzzy picture? One thing remains constant through it all: teachers can and will continue to make a difference in the lives of students.

MAKING A DIFFERENCE BY BEING A DIFFERENT TEACHER

Observing today's more veteran public school teachers in action brings a near-immediate contrast that classroom access to technology in many schools is either sparse or that it exists and utilized far too little within the context of the school day. There is a persistent notion among veteran teachers that smart technology in the hands of the students remains more a novelty than a tool for learning. Teachers teach, and some view smartphones as distractions even as students use them within the learning environment.

Gen Z claims to be the master of multitasking. Others make this same claim about this generation. If this is true, then teachers are going to have to receive proper technology training to prepare for their students. Therefore there must be a philosophical shift from traditional teacher training that broadens the use of technology into their programs. If real reform is to occur in America's public schools, then districts and state departments of education are going to have to require teachers to be certified in educational technology and probably applications too.

Few teachers in the education sphere use technology beyond laptop computers and generic research on smartphones in the classroom. Access to newer technology is often limited in inner-city schools or schools awash in Title I dollars. Career technical education notwithstanding, the majority of students in America with technology access are probably working with laptops and cell phones.

All things considered, one of the main reasons for disconnects between teachers and students over technology is the issue of time. With already diminished classroom instructional time, some states are adding more programs and increasing academic expectations, including greater focus on students with special needs being mainstreamed, second-language learners, and groups of already low achievers. Such expectations make classroom time difficult to muster, given what has been added to the workload plates of teachers—especially at the elementary levels.

Somewhere between the in-services at the beginning of school years, often accompanied by the excitement of motivational speakers and the expectations of administrators in districts, motivation to learn and incorporate technology as education gets lost in the deficit of passion for teaching and learning, the diminished energy levels, and the defaulting to the ease of routines in classrooms. Intentions and reality are time-bound and certainly rely on the same time clock. Schools need to get serious about carving out time for technology use by students. Gen Z expects this during their school day.

General Teaching Styles

The imperative for teachers in American public schools is to know themselves well and to understand their personalities and styles of communicating. Teaching styles are not the same as teaching methods. A method is the vehicle. A style is an approach to the vehicle or how it is to be driven. A lesson plan is like a car. Anyone can drive both. Yet how it is driven brings many images to mind.

Certainly, there is importance in considering whether a teacher is an authoritarian figure, eliciting fear among students. Other considerations should be given to whether a teacher is extremely low key and passive, giving in to students because of his or her fear of not being friendly. Lessons communicated in an authoritarian style may have their place in some content areas on given days. Coaches understand this best. But teachers must adjust the ways the lessons are presented if students are going to maximize learning. This may mean placing the sage on a stage into hiatus or putting the drill sergeant on vacation or even into retirement.

Suggested Teaching Styles

Decades in the classroom do afford teachers some insights across generations. Insights are sometimes best gained by listening and watching. What do Gen Z students think about styles of teaching that work best with them? First, the research is clear that Gen Z students do not enjoy traditional lectures. High schools where teachers still practice the lecture method tied to the teaching style are missing out on maximizing student attentiveness and eventual learning of content. The reality is that Gen Z students of all ages demand more than a lecture these days. Unfortunately, when Gen Z heads off to college, either professors or Gen Z college students or both are going to have to make serious adjustments to their styles.

The fact that Gen Z students will have played about 30,000 hours of video games, online and on their devices, means that their brains are wired differently than those instructing them in their classrooms.[29] Gen Z would prefer a style of teaching that incorporates video games, some visual stimuli, and other interactive elements. They learn better through play because play is fun and engaging. If this play involves many senses, then Gen Z is more apt to learn. Teachers making creative use of this shift in learning styles may have altered their teaching styles.

Another style of teaching is transmitted through collaborative stations or networks. These can be established within the classroom or outside the classroom. They can extend to the community or reach around the world. Gen Z prefers to work collaboratively by the use of digital media, online podcasts, social media, and even blogging. For example, Google tools are wonderful access points to enhance student learning. Used properly by teachers, Google Classroom and "A Google A Day" are intriguing tools to accomplish collaborative efforts.[30]

Digital learning leads to a very important point. Gen Z enjoys learning through self-discovery, and the online world is just a few clicks away. Such technological power makes student learning possible in ways, for example, that a traditional lecturer probably cannot match. A wonderful group of websites that tailor their approaches to Gen Z learning styles, especially in lower grades, are found with Learn Pop: Teachers Pay Teachers (TpT).[31] Created by a former New York City teacher, the sites and links are mostly game related and interactive to meet students' learning needs on a multitude of topics. Teacher collaboration across the globe has enhanced Gen Z learning.[32] One of the benefits of learning through gaming is the security it builds in students taking risks without general fears of embarrassment.

It is not enough to just use technology in the classroom. Incumbent on the teacher is to use technology creatively and effectively. Some teachers are reporting that their Gen Z students are becoming bored with using technology in the classrooms. Again, this comes back to style of teaching. If computers and smartphone devices begin to take on similar feelings derived from teachers giving classroom lectures, the medium will be viewed similarly. Technology is the medium. Lesson plans must take this medium into consideration. Teachers face difficult challenges today now that technology is no longer the novelty it once was. An entire generation is now used to it and knows no time before its existence.[33]

Working against Progress

Even the best planning and most well-executed lessons are overrun by absentees, make-up work, and class academic pull outs. There is "no doubt that finding time to integrate technology is an overwhelming task for anyone. Throughout the course of the days, teachers find themselves pulled in many directions."[34] So using technology regularly, some might conclude, means many students are missing the opportunity to learn. However, "how do educators find an ideal balance for learning about and eventually integrating"[35] qualitative educational technologies into the daily classroom regimen? Each school has different needs and has to consider establishing its own vision for technology.

There is a stark contrast in our schools today. Students are coming with high levels of technology expertise. They expect to remain wired and have access to their daily regimen of social networks. While these could pose a problem for teachers logistically, many of our schools are living in the past, losing their students' interests, and just praying their overhead projector bulbs do not burn out during any given lesson.

Finding the Balance between Technology and Teaching

The twenty-first-century employment picture is going to require some marketable skill sets involving technology.[36] Being able to juggle several projects at the same time is critically important. This happens to be the way Gen Z is wired. "Gone are the days of falling into a profession and riding the wave for 30-plus years."[37]

In terms of literacy, "Along with digital and information literacy skill sets, it's still vital that we promote and encourage a love of reading across all formats—along with a facility for questioning, analyzing, discerning and synthesizing with other media,"[38] all of which Gen Z will need for their entry into the twenty-first-century marketplace to compete. The bottom line is that educational technology is not about "how many apps we integrate, but about providing our students for their futures, not ours."[39]

Is it any wonder that meta-analyses yield what has already been quite sensible to those in the education profession? Peter Greene addresses the question of the veteran teacher in his article "Maybe Old Teachers Don't Stink."[40] The Learning Policy Institute released a meta-analysis—a fancy way to state someone studied studies and drew conclusions—and in the analysis there were four major findings and three recommendations provided by the authors.

Tara Kini and Anne Podolsky found: 1) Additional years of experience for teachers raise students' achievements over the courses of their careers in the classroom. 2) Students attend school more often with veteran teachers and subsequently achieve higher results on assessments as a result. 3) Teachers who collaborate by department, content area, or by grade level find their effectiveness in the classroom improves over time. 4) Mentoring of younger teachers is a plus because veteran teachers increase the level of expertise and incentivize younger teachers to pursue excellence.[41] Indeed, old teachers do not stink. They can be a vibrant asset and add knowledge and wisdom in successfully partnering with the recent Gen Z college grad.

The authors recommend that schools come up with a system to keep veteran teachers employed longer, create a significant and powerful atmosphere that validates professionalism and perpetuates collegiality, and examine how staffing affects the schools of greater needs, such as those in the inner cities and lower socioeconomic areas.[42]

CONCLUSION

Gen Z students would benefit from veteran teachers sticking around, just like other generations benefited from their previous generations. The research studies seem to imply "teachers generally age like fine wine or the stinky cheese . . . and it would strengthen the educational system to encourage the teacher pool to age long and well."[43] That being said, it is imperative that teachers gain the necessary proficiencies to be successful over the long haul. Success with Gen Z requires this acquisition of technology skills.

Teachers may find that Gen Z learning is best accomplished by using the social media with which students are so familiar. Smartphones and other devices can be assets in classrooms and successful learning. In order for some teachers to realize this success, they must become distractors of the distractions facing Gen Z daily.

Making a difference with Gen Z can be accomplished by any teacher, of any age, and with one year in the classroom or thirty years. Longevity in the teaching profession is based on multiple factors. One of these factors is the style employed by teachers to engage students toward learning.

All things considered, working with Gen Z is a privilege. They come with technology savvy and love both independent work and collaborative assignments. The key for every teacher of Gen Z is to remain informed about the cutting-edge technologies available and of course the apps that command the attention of Gen Z students. Success with Gen Z depends on staying informed and discovering the benefits of resilience and flexibility as teachers, focused on a collegial common mission: the success of Gen Z students.

Notes

1. STUDENTS THEN AND NOW

1. Thomas Jefferson, "Letter to William Roscoe," Library of Congress: L&B, 15:303 *polygraph copy*, December 27, 1820, retrieved July 20, 2016, https://www.monticello.org/site/jefferson/follow-truth-quotation Cf. "The Writings of Thomas Jefferson," *Hath Trust Digital Library*, retrieved July 20, 2016, https://catalog.hathitrust.org/Record/006664301
2. Staff, "Education," *Gender Spectrum*, 2015, retrieved November 3, 2016, https://www.genderspectrum.org/explore-topics/education/
3. Richard B. Corradi, "Psychiatry Professor: 'Transgenderism' Is Mass Hysteria Similar to 1980s-Era Junk Science," *Federalist*, November 17, 2016, retrieved November 18, 2016, http://thefederalist.com/2016/11/17/psychiatry-professor-transgenderism-mass-hysteria-similar-1980s-era-junk-science/
4. Suzannah Weiss, "An Anti-LGBTQ Law in Texas Could Force Teachers to Out Kids," *Glamour*, November 21, 2016, retrieved November 22, 2016, http://www.glamour.com/story/an-anti-lgbtq-law-in-texas-could-force-teachers-to-out-kids
5. Alyson Klein, "Obama Administration Releases Final Testing Regulations for ESSA," *Education Week*, December 7, 2016, retrieved December 9, 2016, http://blogs.edweek.org/edweek/campaign-k-12/2016/12/obama_administration_releases_.html
6. Weiss, "An Anti-LGBTQ Law in Texas Could Force Teachers to Out Kids."
7. Katherine Timpf, "School Told to Call Kids 'Purple Penguins' Because 'Boys and Girls' Is Not Inclusive to Transgender," *National Review*, October 8, 2014, retrieved September 5, 2016, http://www.nationalreview.com/article/389862/school-told-call-kids-purple-penguins-because-boys-and-girls-not-inclusive
8. Staff, "Education."
9. Lane Brown, "Gender Neutrality: Why Teachers Won't Ask Boys and Girls to Line Up in Lincoln, Neb.," *Christian Science Monitor*, October 9, 2016, retrieved November 22, 2016, http://www.csmonitor.com/The-Culture/Family/Modern-Parenthood/2014/1009/Gender-neutrality-Why-teachers-won-t-ask-boys-and-girls-to-line-up-in-Lincoln-Neb

10. Todd Starnes, "NC School to Teachers: Don't Call Students 'Boys and Girls,'" *Fox News*, August 16, 2016, retrieved November 22, 2016, http://www.foxnews.com/opinion/2016/08/16/nc-school-to-teachers-dont-call-students-boys-and-girls.html

11. Timpf, "School Told to Call Kids 'Purple Penguins' Because 'Boys and Girls' Is Not Inclusive to Transgender."

12. Staff, "Education."

13. Jim Taylor, "Technology: Is Technology Stealing Our (Self) Identities?" *Psychology Today*, July 27, 2011, retrieved November 10, 2016, https://www.psychologytoday.com/blog/the-power-prime/201107/technology-is-technology-stealing-our-self-identities

14. Ibid.

15. Ernest J. Zarra III, *The Wrong Direction for Today's Schools: The Impact of Common Core upon American Education* (Lanham, MD: Rowman & Littlefield, 2015).

16. Staff, "Annual Sleep in America Poll Exploring Connections with Communications Technology Use and Sleep," *National Sleep Foundation*, March 7, 2011, retrieved November 7, 2016, https://sleepfoundation.org/media-center/press-release/annual-sleep-america-poll-exploring-connections-communications-technology-use-

17. Tawnell D. Hobbs, "U.S. Teenagers Lose Ground in International Math Exam, Raising Competitiveness Concerns," *Wall Street Journal*, December 6, 2016, retrieved December 8, 2016, http://www.wsj.com/articles/u-s-teenagers-lose-ground-in-international-math-exam-raising-competitiveness-concerns-1481018401

18. Andrew J. Rotherham, "School Districts Do Too Much," *U.S. News & World Report*, July 5, 2016, retrieved July 18, 2016, http://www.usnews.com/opinion/articles/2016-07-05/let-school-districts-focus-on-instruction

19. Ibid.

20. George Beall, "8 Key Differences between Gen Z and Millennials," *Huffington Post*, November 5, 2016, retrieved November 7, 2016, http://www.huffingtonpost.com/george-beall/8-key-differences-between_b_12814200.html

21. Ibid.

22. Ibid.

23. Rotherham, "School Districts Do Too Much."

24. Amanda Claire Curcio, "Teen Fails to Make Cheerleader, Threatens to Sue," *USA Today*, July 18, 2016, retrieved July 18, 2016, http://www.usatoday.com/story/news/nation-now/2016/07/18/cheerleading-lawsuit-threat/87260174/

25. Ibid.

26. Neil Howe and William Strauss, *Millennials Rising: The Next Great Generation* (New York: Vantage Books, 2000), 42–43.

27. Susan Edelman, "High School's New Policy Would Allow Failing Students to Pass," *New York Post*, July 17, 2016, retrieved July 17, 2016, http://nypost.com/2016/07/17/high-schools-new-policy-would-allow-failing-students-to-pass/

28. Curcio, "Teen Fails to Make Cheerleader, Threatens to Sue."

29. Tom Knighton, "Spoiled College Grad Demands New Dress Code at Job, Gets the Boot," *P. J. Media*, June 29, 2016, retrieved July 18, 2016, https://pjmedia.com/trending/2016/06/29/spoiled-college-grad-demands-new-dress-code-at-job-gets-the-boot/

30. Bre Payton, "University Investigates Professor for Encouraging Debate," *Federalist*, June 21, 2016, retrieved June 22, 2016, http://thefederalist.com/2016/06/21/university-investigates-professor-for-encouraging-debate/

31. Knighton, "Spoiled College Grad Demands New Dress Code at Job, Gets the Boot."

32. Jonathan Haidt, "The Coddling of the American Mind," *Atlantic*, September 2015, retrieved June 22, 2016, 1, http://www.theatlantic.com/magazine/archive/2015/09/the-coddling-of-the-american-mind/399356/.
33. Ibid., 2.
34. Ibid., 12.
35. Ibid.
36. Ibid., 12–13.
37. Ibid., 3.
38. Ibid., 12–14.
39. Ibid., 8–9.
40. Ibid., 5.
41. Ibid., 4.
42. Ibid., 13.
43. David D. Burns, *Feeling Good: The New Mood Therapy* (New York: HarperCollins, 1999), 12.
44. Robert L. Leahy, Stephen J. F. Holland, and Lata McGinn, *Treatment Plans and Interventions for Depression and Anxiety Disorders*, 2nd ed. (London: Guilford Press, 2012), 16–26.
45. Haidt, "The Coddling of the American Mind," 15.
46. Ibid., 10.
47. Ibid.
48. Ibid., 12.

2. ARE GEN Z STUDENTS SMARTER THAN THEIR TECHNOLOGY?

1. Ernest J. Zarra III, *Common Sense Education: From Common Core to ESSA and Beyond* (Lanham, MD: Rowman & Littlefield Publishers, 2016).
2. Barack Obama, "College for All: Is Obama's Goal Attainable?" NBC News, February 28, 2009, retrieved December 10, 2016, http://www.nbcnews.com/id/29445201/ns/us_news-education/t/college-all-obamas-goal-attainable/#.WEv6RvkrKUk
3. Staff, "ACT/SAT Optional College List Soars to 280," *Fair Test: The National Center for Fair and Open Testing*, 2016, retrieved November 23, 2016, http://www.fairtest.org/act-sat-optional-colleges-list-soars-280
4. Zarra, *Common Sense Education*.
5. Jeff Guo, "Why College Students Who Do Well in High School Bomb in College," *Washington Post*, September 21, 2016, retrieved September 25, 2016, https://www.washingtonpost.com/news/wonk/wp/2016/09/21/why-students-who-do-well-in-high-school-bomb-in-college/
6. Ibid.
7. Ibid.
8. Ibid.
9. Ibid.
10. Ibid.
11. Ibid.

12. J. Chamberlin, "Study Reveals Startling Abuse of Teachers by Students, Even Parents," *American Psychological Association* 41, no. 9 (October 2010): 13, retrieved November 15, 2016, http://www.apa.org/monitor/2010/10/teachers.aspx

13. Staff, "Students Bullying Teachers: A New Epidemic," *No Bullying.com*, October 18, 2016, retrieved November 15, 2016, https://nobullying.com/students-bullying-teachers-a-new-epidemic/

14. Melanie Ehrenkranz, "Hacked Slack Discussion Reveals Teachers Saying Horrible Things about Their Students," *AOL News*, June 24, 2016, retrieved November 15, 2016, http://www.aol.com/article/2016/06/24/hacked-slack-discussion-reveals-teachers-say-horrible-things-about-students/21401654/

15. Sarah Larimer, "Teachers Insulted Students in Private Slack Chats. After a Hack, They Resigned in Disgrace," *Washington Post*, June 24, 2016, retrieved November 15, 2016, https://www.washingtonpost.com/news/education/wp/2016/06/24/teachers-insulted-students-in-private-slack-chats-after-a-hack-they-resigned-in-disgrace/?utm_source=AOL&utm_medium=readMore&utm_campaign=partner

16. Staff, "Students Bullying Teachers."

17. Ibid.

18. Ibid.

19. Joel Hartman, Patsy Moskal, and Chuck Dziuban, "Educating the Net Generation: Preparing the Academy of Today for the Learner of Tomorrow," *EDUCAUSE*, 2016, retrieved July 21, 2016, http://www.educause.edu/research-and-publications/books/educating-net-generation/preparing-academy-today-learner-tomorrow

20. Martin L. Kutscher and Natalie Rosin, "Too Much Screen Time? When Your Child with ADHD Over-Connects to Technology," *Children and Adults with Attention-Deficit/Hyperactivity Disorder (CHADD)*, June 2015, 22–25, retrieved November 12, 2016, http://www.chadd.org/AttentionPDFs/ATTN_06_15_TooMuchScreenTime.pdf

21. Ibid.

22. Daniel Goleman, *Social Intelligence: The Revolutionary New Science of Human Relationships* (New York: Random House, 2006), 181–82.

23. Ibid.

24. Michael J. Petrilli, "Kid, I'm Sorry, but You're Just Not College Material," *Slate*, March 14, 2014, retrieved October 30, 2016, http://www.slate.com/articles/life/education/2014/03/college_isn_t_for_everyone_let_s_stop_pretending_it_is.html

25. Barack Obama, "President Obama Delivers Remarks on Education," *YouTube*, October 17, 2016, retrieved October 27, 2016, https://www.youtube.com/watch?v=dqHz33Q9XC4

26. Ibid.

27. Ibid. Cf. Melanie Garunay, "As Graduation Rate Reaches New High, One Student Shares His Story," *White House*, October 17, 2016, retrieved October 27, 2016, https://www.whitehouse.gov/blog/2016/10/17/graduation-rate-reaches-new-high-one-student-shares-his-story

28. Adam Renfro, "Meet Generation Z," *EdTech Getting Smart*, December 5, 2012, retrieved August 4, 2016, http://gettingsmart.com/2012/12/meet-generation-z/

29. Ibid.

30. Hayley Peterson, "Millennials Are Old News—Here's Everything You Should Know about Generation Z," *Business Insider*, June 25, 2014, retrieved August 5, 2016, http://www.businessinsider.com/generation-z-spending-habits-2014-6.

31. C. S. Lewis, *The Four Loves* (New York: Harcourt Brace, 1960).

32. Goleman, *Social Intelligence*, 83.

33. Shelly Kramer, "The Demographic Tsunami to Come: The Spending Habits of Gen Z," *Digitalist*, January 8, 2016, retrieved August 5, 2016, http://www.digitalistmag.com/customer-experience/2016/01/08/spending-habits-of-Gen Z-03927717

34. Grace L. Williams, "Generation Z to Eclipse Millennials as Economic Force, Says Goldman Sachs," *Today*, December 4, 2015, retrieved August 5, 2016, http://www.today.com/money/generation-z-eclipse-millennials-economic-force-says-goldman-sachs-t59436 Cf. Joy-Ann Reid, "For Gen Z, Bernie Sanders Answers the 'How' of Policy-Making," MSNBC, February 1, 2016, retrieved August 5, 2016, http://www.msnbc.com/msnbc/Gen Z-bernie-sanders-answers-the-how-policy-making

35. Kramer, "The Demographic Tsunami to Come."

36. Ipsos Media CT, "Generation Z: A Look at the Technology and Media Habits of Today's Teens," *Wikia*, March 19, 2013, retrieved August 28, 2016, http://www.prnewswire.com/news-releases/generation-z-a-look-at-the-technology-and-media-habits-of-todays-teens-198958011.html

37. Ibid.

38. Janna Anderson, "Main Findings: Teens, Technology, and Human Potential in 2020," Pew Research Center, February 29, 2012, retrieved November 20, 2016, http://www.pewinternet.org/2012/02/29/main-findings-teens-technology-and-human-potential-in-2020/

39. Ibid.

40. Ibid.

41. Ibid.

42. "Meet Generation Z: Marketing & Attention Span," CBS News, 2016, retrieved August 11, 2016, http://www.cbsnews.com/pictures/meet-generation-z/16/

43. Ibid.

3. TEACHING TO ENGAGE GEN Z

1. Patrick Deneen, "Professor Patrick Deneen Explains How Kids Have Become a Generation of Know-Nothings," *Signs of the Times*, February 2, 2016, retrieved July 7, 2016, https://www.sott.net/article/312948-Professor-Patrick-Deneen-explains-how-kids-have-become-a-generation-of-know-nothings

2. Valerie Strauss, "What the Modern World Has Forgotten about Children and Learning," *Washington Post*, August 19, 2016, retrieved August 23, 2016, https://www.washingtonpost.com/news/answer-sheet/wp/2016/08/19/what-the-modern-world-has-forgotten-about-children-and-learning/

3. La Monica Everett-Haynes, "Trending Now: Generation Z," *UA News: The University of Arizona*, November 8, 2013, retrieved November 20, 2016, https://uanews.arizona.edu/blog/trending-now-Generation Z

4. Robert Earl, "Do Cell Phones Belong in the Classroom?" *Atlantic*, May 18, 2012, retrieved November 20, 2016, http://www.theatlantic.com/national/archive/2012/05/do-cell-phones-belong-in-the-classroom/257325/

5. Staff, "New Vision for Education: Fostering Social and Emotional Learning through Technology," World Economic Forum, in Collaboration with the Boston Group, March 2016, retrieved October 14, 2016, http://www3.weforum.org/docs/WEF_New_Vision_for_Education.pdf

6. Ibid.

7. Ibid.
8. Ibid.
9. Ibid.
10. Ibid.
11. Mary Helen Immordino-Yang, *Emotions, Learning, and the Brain: Exploring the Educational Implications of Affective Neuroscience* (New York: W. W. Norton & Company, 2015), 18–20.
12. Ibid., 18.
13. Mark McCrindle, "Learning Styles," *Generation Z Blog*, October 18, 2016, retrieved October 18, 2016, http://generationz.com.au/learning-styles/
14. Jordana Cepelewicz, "How Your Brain Learns Physics," *Scientific American*, August 1, 2016, retrieved August 2, 2016, http://www.scientificamerican.com/article/how-your-brain-learns-physics/
15. Ibid.
16. Donna Wilson, "Strategies for Strengthening the Brain's Executive Functions," *Edutopia*, April 2, 2015, retrieved June 24, 2016, http://www.edutopia.org/blog/strategies-strengthening-brains-executive-functions-donna-wilson-marcus-conyers
17. Staff, "Gen Z on Social Media," *Inflexion Interactive*, July 7, 2015, retrieved August 11, 2016, https://inflexioninteractive.com/Gen Z-social-media-apps/
18. Nathan McAlone and Alex Heath, "The 16 Social Media Apps Everyone Should Have," *Business Insider*, November 14, 2015, retrieved August 11, 2016, http://www.businessinsider.com/best-social-media-apps-2015-11/#facebook-messenger-is-becoming-the-one-app-to-rule-them-all-1
19. "Meet Generation Z: Digital Privacy," CBS News, 2016, retrieved August 11, 2016, http://www.cbsnews.com/pictures/meet-Generation Z/8/
20. "Meet Generation Z: Snapchat," CBS News, 2016, retrieved August 11, 2016, http://www.cbsnews.com/pictures/meet-Generation Z/9/
21. Ernest J. Zarra III, *Teacher-Student Relationships: Crossing into the Emotional, Physical, and Sexual Realms* (Lanham, MD: Rowman & Littlefield Publishers, 2013), 75–97.
22. Doug Lemov, *Teach Like a Champion* (San Francisco, CA: Jossey-Bass, 2010), 167–77.
23. Ben Johnson, "The 5 Priorities of Classroom Management," *Edutopia*, September 2, 2016, retrieved November 26, 2016, https://www.edutopia.org/blog/5-priorities-classroom-management-ben-johnson.
24. Wilson, "Strategies for Strengthening the Brain's Executive Functions."
25. Ibid.
26. Ibid.
27. Judy Willis, "Building Brain Literacy in Elementary Students," *Edutopia*, November 19, 2013, retrieved June 24, 2016, http://www.edutopia.org/blog/building-brain-literacy-elementary-students-judy-willis
28. Diane Oblinger, "Boomers, Gen-Xers, and Millennials: Understanding the New Students," *Educause Review* 4, no. 38 (July/August 2003): 36–40, 42, 44–45, retrieved August 13, 2016, http://www.odec.umd.edu/CD/AGE/MILLEN.PDF
29. Ibid., 40–41.
30. Ibid.
31. Ibid.
32. Ibid.

33. Alex Williams, "Move Over, Millennials, Here Comes Generation Z," *New York Times*, September 18. 2015, retrieved July 7, 2016, http://www.nytimes.com/2015/09/20/fashion/move-over-millennials-here-comes-Generation Z.html

34. Diane Smith and Monica S. Nagy, "Meet the Class of 2018: Digitally Fluent Gen Z." *Star-Telegram*, September 1, 2014, retrieved July 4, 2016, http://www.star-telegram.com/news/local/education/article3871560.html

35. Phil Parker, "Do You Know How Generation Z Pupils Learn?" *SecEd*, May 2, 2013, retrieved August 5, 2016, http://www.sec-ed.co.uk/blog/do-you-know-how-Generation Z-pupils-learn/ Cf. Adam Renfro, "Understanding the Generation Z Student," *Virtual School Alliance*, January 13, 2015, retrieved August 5, 2016, http://www.virtualschoolalliance.org/understanding-Generation Z-student/

36. Tiffany Ford, "5 Tips for Teaching Generation Z in College" *Tophat Blog*, November 25, 2015, retrieved October 3, 2016, https://blog.tophat.com/generation-z/

37. Sarah Fudin, "Gen Z and What Does It Mean in Your Classroom?" *University of Southern California (SCRossierOnline)*, March 29, 2012, retrieved July 7, 2016, https://rossieronline.usc.edu/Gen Z-what-does-it-mean-in-your-classroom-2/

38. Alexandra Levit, "The Future of Education According to Generation Z," *Time*, April 6, 2015, retrieved July 7, 2016, http://time.com/3764545/future-of-education/

39. Ibid.

40. Ford, "5 Tips for Teaching Generation Z in College."

41. Levit, "The Future of Education According to Generation Z."

42. Fudin, "Gen Z and What Does It Mean in Your Classroom?"

43. Dan Henderson, *That's Special: A Survival Guide to Teaching* (Denver: Outskirts Press, 2015).

44. Peter Greene, "Maybe Old Teachers Don't Stink," *Huffington Post*, June 10, 2016, retrieved June 11, 2016, http://www.huffingtonpost.com/peter-greene/maybe-old-teachers-dont-s_b_10404600.html

45. Ford, "5 Tips for Teaching Generation Z in College."

46. Johnson, "The 5 Priorities of Classroom Management."

47. Ibid.

48. Ibid.

49. Ford, "5 Tips for Teaching Generation Z in College."

50. Johnson, "The 5 Priorities of Classroom Management."

51. Emily Ram, "The Newsies!: Teacher Survey Reveals Cell Phone Problems," *New York Daily News*, December 10, 2015, retrieved November 20, 2016, http://www.nydailynews.com/new-york/education/teacher-survey-reveals-issues-cell-phones-classes-article-1.2452229

52. Ibid.

53. Lemov, *Teach Like a Champion*, 150–53.

54. Ted Powers, "Engaging Students with Humor," *Association for Psychological Science*, December 5, 2005, retrieved November 20, 2016, http://www.psychologicalscience.org/observer/engaging-students-with-humor#.WDHJMfkrKUk

55. Ibid.

56. Ford, "5 Tips for Teaching Generation Z in College."

57. Ibid.

58. Jacob Morgan, "Generation Z and the 6 Forces Shaping the Future of Business," *Inc*, July 5, 2016, retrieved July 21, 2016, http://www.inc.com/jacob-morgan/Generation Z-and-the-6-forces-shaping-the-future-of-business.html

59. Caroline Geck, "The Generation Z Connections: Teaching Information Literacy to the Newest Net Generation," *Teacher Librarian*, 34, no. 3 (February 2006): 239.

60. Ibid., 237.
61. Ibid., 239.
62. Staff, "New Vision for Education."
63. Ibid.
64. David J. Deming, "The Growing Importance of Social Skills in the Labor Market," Harvard University and National Bureau of Economic Research, August 2015, retrieved October 14, 2016, https://scholar.harvard.edu/files/ddeming/files/deming_socialskills_august2015.pdf
65. Staff, "New Vision for Education."
66. Tom Vander Ark, "Getting Smart: How Digital Learning Is Changing the World—2013 Update," *Education Week*, January 1, 2014, retrieved August 4, 2016, http://blogs.edweek.org/edweek/on_innovation/2014/01/getting_smart_how_digital_learning_is_changing_the_world_2013_update.html
67. Brian Mastroianni, "How Generation Z Is Changing the Tech World," CBS News, March 10, 2016, retrieved August 4, 2016, http://www.cbsnews.com/news/social-media-fuels-a-change-in-generations-with-the-rise-of-Gen Z/
68. Ford, "5 Tips for Teaching Generation Z in College."
69. Marilyn Price-Mitchell, "Curiosity: The Force within a Hungry Mind," *Edutopia*, February 17, 2016, retrieved August 5, 2016, http://www.edutopia.org/blog/8-pathways-curiosity-hungry-mind-marilyn-price-mitchell
70. Grace Tatter, "Tennessee to Become National Pioneer in Creating Social and Emotional Standards," *Chalk Beat*, August 3, 2016, retrieved August 7, 2016, http://www.chalkbeat.org/posts/tn/2016/08/03/tennessee-to-become-national-pioneer-in-creating-social-and-emotional-standards/#.V7RIjpgrKUk
71. Ibid.

4. EXPECTATIONS OF GEN Z STUDENTS

1. Jan Hoffman, "As Attention Grows, Transgender Children's Numbers Are Elusive," *New York Times*, May 17, 2016, retrieved November 13, 2016, http://www.nytimes.com/2016/05/18/science/transgender-children.html
2. David Cortman, "Is Anyone Else Getting Tired of This Whole Politically Correct Bullying Thing?" *Townhall*, January 22, 2012, retrieved November 23, 2016, http://townhall.com/columnists/davidcortman/2012/01/22/is_anyone_else_getting_tired_of_this_whole_politically_correct_bullying_thing Cf. Jane Ridley, "The 5 Most Outrageous Politically Correct School Rules," *New York Post*, March 27, 2015, retrieved October 4, 2016, http://nypost.com/2015/03/27/the-5-most-outrageous-politically-correct-school-rules/
3. Todd Starnes, "NC School to Teachers: Don't Call Student 'Boys and Girls,'" Fox News, August 16, 2016, retrieved November 13, 2016, http://www.foxnews.com/opinion/2016/08/16/nc-school-to-teachers-dont-call-students-boys-and-girls.html
4. Hannah Fingerhut, "Support Steady for Same-Sex Marriage and Acceptance of Homosexuality," Pew Research Center, May 12, 2016, retrieved November 13, 2016, http://www.pewresearch.org/fact-tank/2016/05/12/support-steady-for-same-sex-marriage-and-acceptance-of-homosexuality/

5. Staff, "GLAAD Media Reference Guide: Terms to Avoid," Gay and Lesbian Alliance against Defamation (GLAAD), 2016, retrieved November 13, 2016, http://www.glaad.org/reference/offensive

6. Ibid.

7. Leif Mitchell and Meredith Startz, "Tackling LGBT Issues in School," Gay, Lesbian and Straight Education Network (GLSEN), 2007, retrieved November 13, 2016, https://www.glsen.org/sites/default/files/GLSEN%20CT%20Tackling%20LGBT%20Issues%20In%20Schools.pdf

8. Kevin Liptak, "Obama Questions on LGBT Rights, Black Lives Matter in London," CNN, April 23, 2016, retrieved November 13, 2016, http://www.cnn.com/2016/04/23/politics/obama-london-town-hall/

9. Staff, "Feelings Now Acceptable as Answers to Math Problems," *Babylon Bee*, October 3, 2016, retrieved October 8, 2016, http://babylonbee.com/news/feelings-now-acceptable-answers-math-problems/

10. Charles C. W. Cooke, "The Left Realizes Too Late That Political Correctness Is a Virus," *National Review*, January 30, 2015, retrieved September 25, 2016, http://www.nationalreview.com/article/397613/left-realizes-too-late-political-correctness-virus-charles-c-w-cooke

11. Joseph Stiglitz, "Equal Opportunity, Our National Myth," *New York Times*, February 16, 2013, retrieved December 11, 2016, http://opinionator.blogs.nytimes.com/2013/02/16/equal-opportunity-our-national-myth/?_r=0. Cf. Office of the Press Secretary, "Fact Sheet: President Obama Announces High School Graduation Rate Has Reached New High," The White House, October 17, 2016, retrieved October 23, 2016, https://www.whitehouse.gov/the-press-office/2016/10/17/fact-sheet-president-obama-announces-high-school-graduation-rate-has

12. Thomas Sowell, "The Fallacy of Equating Differences in Outcomes with Differences in Opportunity," *National Review*, September 16, 2015, retrieved December 11, 2016, http://www.nationalreview.com/article/424051/fallacy-equating-differences-outcome-differences-opportunity-thomas-sowell

13. Robert Gehl, "Top Ten New Offensive Words You Can't Use Anymore," *Downtrend*, March 13, 2014, retrieved November 13, 2016, http://downtrend.com/robertgehl/top-ten-new-offensive-words-you-cant-use-anymore

14. Lydia Murray, "Conservative Author Ben Shapiro Talks Free Speech, Microaggression," *Michigan Daily*, April 7, 2016, retrieved November 19, 2016, https://www.michigandaily.com/section/news/ben-shapiro-talks-truth-microaggression

15. Jeffrey J. Sellingo, "Helicopter Parents Are Not the Only Problem. Colleges Coddle Students Too," *Washington Post*, October 21, 2015, retrieved November 19, 2016, https://www.washingtonpost.com/news/grade-point/wp/2015/10/21/helicopter-parents-are-not-the-only-problem-colleges-coddle-students-too/. Cf. Kathleen Elliott Vinson, "Hovering Too Close: The Ramifications of Helicopter Parenting," University of Houston Law Center, 2011, 11–26, retrieved November 19, 2016, https://www.law.uh.edu/ihelg/monograph/11-12.pdf

16. Pat Morrison, "How 'Helicopter Parenting' Is Ruining America's Children," *Los Angeles Times*, October 28, 2015, retrieved November 19, 2016, http://www.latimes.com/opinion/op-ed/la-oe-morrison-lythcott-haims-20151028-column.html

17. Nancy Gibbs, "The Growing Backlash against Overparenting," *Time*, November 30, 2009, retrieved November 19, 2016, http://www.time.com/time/magazine/article/0,9171,1940697,00.html

18. Staff, "Millennials on Steroids: Is Your Brand Ready for Generation Z?" Wharton School of Business at UPenn, September 28, 2015, retrieved August 5, 2016, http://knowledge.wharton.upenn.edu/article/millennials-on-steroids-is-your-brand-ready-for-generation-z/
19. Dan Schawbel, *Promote Yourself* (New York: St. Martin's Press, 2013), 156.
20. Staff, "Millennials on Steroids."
21. Mallory Schlossberg, "Teen Generation Z Is Being Called 'Millennials on Steroids,' and That Could Be Terrifying for Retailers," *Business Insider*, February 11, 2016, retrieved August 5, 2016, http://www.businessinsider.com/millennials-vs-Gen Z-2016-2
22. Schawbel, *Promote Yourself*, 156.
23. Ibid.
24. Rachel Gillett, "A Former Harvard Admissions Interviewer Shares the 4 Skills Everyone Should Have by Age 18," *Business Insider*, November 13, 2016, retrieved November 13, 2016, https://amp.businessinsider.com/ex-harvard-interviewer-shares-life-skills-everyone-should-have-2016-11
25. Ibid.
26. "Generation Z and Money Survey: Understanding Tomorrow's Investors," TD Ameritrade, June 20, 2012, retrieved August 10, 2016, http://s1.q4cdn.com/959385532/files/doc_news/research/GenZandMoneyFindingFINAL-standard.pdf
27. Ibid.
28. Ibid.
29. Ibid.
30. Ibid.
31. Ibid.
32. "24 Actual Things Parents Said to Teachers That Will Make Your Head Spin," *Topix: Offbeat*, 2016, retrieved July 9, 2016, http://offbeat.topix.com/slideshow/16097/slide1

5. SUCCESS WITH GEN Z

1. Andrew Marcinek, "Technology and Teaching: Finding a Balance," *Edutopia*, March 11, 2014, retrieved June 24, 2016, http://www.edutopia.org/blog/technology-and-teaching-finding-balance-andrew-marcinek
2. Kimberlee Morrison, "How Is Gen Z Using Social Media?" Infographic: Let's Get Social, *Social Times*, March 24, 2016, retrieved August 7, 2016, http://www.adweek.com/socialtimes/how-is-Gen Z-using-social-media/636574
3. Ibid.
4. Ibid.
5. Aubrey Andrus, "Gen Z vs. Gen Y: Does the Hype Add Up?" *Sprout Social*, September 1, 2015, http://sproutsocial.com/insights/Gen Z-vs-gen-y/
6. Slack, https://slack.com/
7. Chris Matyszczyk, "Teachers Out at Prep School After Slack Messages about Students Are Revealed," *CNET*, June 26, 2016, retrieved June 26, 2016, http://www.cnet.com/news/teachers-out-at-prep-school-after-nasty-slack-messages-about-students-are-revealed/
8. Sarah Larimer, "Teachers Insulted Students in Private Slack Chats. After a Hack, They Resigned in Disgrace," *Washington Post*, June 24, 2016, retrieved August 14, 2016, https://www.washingtonpost.com/news/education/wp/2016/06/24/teachers-insulted-students-in-private-slack-chats-after-a-hack-they-resigned-in-disgrace/

9. Ibid.

10. Johanna Sorrentino, "Cell Phones: 21st Century Learning Tools? An Interview with Lisa Kolb," *Education.com*, April 2, 2014, retrieved July 18, 2016, http://www.education.com/magazine/article/cell_phone_learning/

11. Bill Alberti, "Still Obsessing Over Millennials? Here Are 6 Rules for Teaching Generation Z," *AdWeek*, May 21, 2015, retrieved August 4, 2016, http://www.adweek.com/news/advertising-branding/still-obsessing-over-millennials-here-are-6-rules-reaching-generation-z-164882

12. Ibid.

13. Alexandra Levit, "The Future of Education According to Generation Z," *Time*, April 6, 2015, retrieved July 18, 2016, http://time.com/3764545/future-of-education/

14. Ibid.

15. Phil Hill, "MOOCs Are Dead. Long Live Online Higher Education," *Chronicle of Higher Education*, August 26, 2016, retrieved August 27, 2016, http://www.chronicle.com/article/MOOCs-Are-Dead-Long-Live/237569

16. Jeffrey R. Young, "Online Education Is Now a Global Market," *Chronicle of Higher Education*, October 5, 2016, retrieved October 6, 2016, http://www.chronicle.com/article/Online-Education-Is-Now-a/237993

17. Levit, "The Future of Education According to Generation Z."

18. Ibid.

19. Ibid.

20. Ibid.

21. Ibid.

22. Alex Williams, "Move Over, Millennials. Here Comes Generation Z," *New York Times*, September 18, 2015, retrieved November 21, 2016, http://www.nytimes.com/2015/09/20/fashion/move-over-millennials-here-comes-generation-z.html

23. Diane Smith and Monica S. Nagy, "Meet the Class of 2018: Digitally Fluent Gen Z," *Star-Telegram*, September 1. 2014, retrieved November 21, 2016, http://www.star-telegram.com/news/local/education/article3871560.html

24. Ford, "5 Tips for Teaching Generation Z in College."

25. Ibid.

26. Levit, "The Future of Education According to Generation Z."

27. Ford, "5 Tips for Teaching Generation Z in College."

28. Levit, "The Future of Education According to Generation Z."

29. Lauren Martin, "How Generation Z Learns," *Learning Liftoff*, May 8, 2014, retrieved October 29, 2016, http://www.learningliftoff.com/generation-z-learns/#.WBTK0PkrKUk

30. Staff, "Teaching Generation Z," *Using Better Technology*, October 25, 2014, retrieved October 29, 2016, http://usingtechnologybetter.com/teaching-generation-z/

31. Paul Edelman (Founder), "About Us," *Teacher Pay Teachers*, retrieved October 29, 2016, https://www.teacherspayteachers.com/About-Us

32. Ibid.

33. Staff, "Teaching Generation Z."

34. Marcinek, "Technology and Teaching."

35. Ibid.

36. Karin Fischer, "The Employment Mismatch," *Chronicle of Higher Education*, March 4, 2013, retrieved July 14, 2016, http://chronicle.com/article/the-employment-mismatch/137625#id=overview

37. Marcinek, "Technology and Teaching."

38. Ibid.

39. Ibid.

40. Peter Greene, "Maybe Old Teachers Don't Stink," *Huffington Post*, June 10, 2016, retrieved June 12, 2016, http://www.huffingtonpost.com/peter-greene/maybe-old-teachers-dont-s_b_10404600.html

41. Tara Kini and Anne Podolsky, "Does Teaching Experience Increase Teacher Effectiveness? A Review of the Research," *Learning Policy Institute*, 2016, retrieved June 12, 2016, https://learningpolicyinstitute.org/our-work/publications-resources/does-teaching-experience-increase-teacher-effectiveness-review-research/

42. Ibid.

43. Greene, "Maybe Old Teachers Don't Stink."

Index

abnormal, 73
abortion, 72
academic achievements, 11
academic assessments, 9
academic rigor, 23
accommodation, 7
ADHD. *See* attention deficit hyperactivity disorder
addicted to devices, xii, 8
advanced placement classes, 62, 105
Akroyd, Dan, 44
Alberti, Bill, 99
alternative education, 33
American families, 41
American College Testing (ACT), 23, 24
American culture, 7; changes in, 71; shapers of, 81; war on, 76
American Dream, 77
Americanism, 7
amygdalae, 61
apps, 49
Asia, 103
Asperger's syndrome, 7
assessments, 9, 23
attention deficit hyperactivity disorder (ADHD), 2, 7, 94
autism spectrum, 2
average daily attendance (ADA), 7

Baby Boomers, 1, 6
Babylon Bee, 74–75

Beattie, Graham, 25
bailed out, 10
bias, 4
biological issues, 94
biochemical abnormalities, 2
bipolar, 3, 94
Black Lives Matter, 35
Bloom's Taxonomy, 51
brain: and technology, 53; chemical changes, 5; development, 3, 5, 8, 45, 48, 49; executive function, 51; making connections, 54
bulldozer parents, 82, 105
Burns, David D., 18
Bush-era, 23

California, 13, 69
California High School Exit Exam (CAHSEE), 13
campus scrubbing, 17
candidacies drive by social media, 35
capitalist, 13
capturing moments, 98
Carnegie Mellon University, 48
Career Technical Education (CTE), 62, 63, 108
causes célèbres, 71
cell phones, 58
Cepelewicz, Jordan, 48
certificate for participation, 24
chalkboards, 7

character, 26, 49
Charlotte, North Carolina, 71
cheerleader, 13
chemical imbalance, 94
Chicago Public Schools, 74
Children and Adults with Attention-Deficit Hyperactivity Disorder (CHADD), 30
civil rights, 5
classroom management: flipped classroom for, 54; smartphone use and, 101; structure and, 57
cognitive awareness, 51
cognitive disorders, 18
Cold War, 7, 19
collaborative groups, 100
college alternatives, 36
college not meant for everyone, 22
college requirements, 23
comedians, 17
committing an offense, 19
Common Core, 9, 54–56, 61, 62, 65, 105, 107; failings of, 23; student readiness for college, 32
competency-based education (CBE), 104
completeness academically, 9
computers, 52
conservative politicians, 76
constant connectivity, 8
creative bullying, 29
creative teachers, 98
critical thinking and lost rigor, 9, 24
crowd sourcing, 35
cultural immunity, 72
cultural marginalization, 71

deceptive digital world, 52
Deming, David, 65
Department of Education (DOE), 17
Department of Justice (DOJ), 17
Descartes, Rene, 46
device addiction and distraction, xii, 8
digital: foreigners, 78, 89; immigrants, 78, 89; integrators, 47, 54; literacy, 27, 89; natives, 78, 89
diplomas for participation, 13
divers, 25
diverse learners, 46
diversity, 46
domestic competition, 9

dopamine, 29
drop out of college, 104
dual enrollment, 32, 104–105
dysfunctions, 2
dysphoria, 71
Dziuban, Chuck, 34–35

Earl, Robert, 42
economic boom, 7
economic fairness, 76–77
economic forecast, 65
education: delivery of, 93; experiment, 6; flipped, 47; grants, 56; less pure, 44; mediocrity, 24; of the whole child, 44; radical changes, 41; their way, 8
educational technology innovations, 49, 103
education and triages, 2
elementary school, 10
emojis, 27
emoticons, 27, 65
emotional reactions, 52
emotional steering mechanism, 46
emotional thermostat, 31
emotions: actions associated with, 19; as motivators, 10; as truth, 18, 19; feelings manifested, 19; focusing on, 12; logic displayed, 19; manipulated by, 9; memories with, 45–46; used as reason, 20; within the classroom, 10
empathy, 53, 106
engaging the distracted, 99
entitlement expectations, 20
Europe, 103
everyone gets a diploma, 57, 84
Every Student Succeeds Act (ESSA), 2, 6, 54, 62, 65, 103, 107
expedition learning, 55
explosive numbers, 2
expressing views, 17

Facebook, 96
Facetime, 27
fake news, 30
faith background, 44
family: customs, 41; nuclear, 41
fatter thumbs, 21
feelings: application of, 3, 10; as secondary, 10; not enough, 12; of

entitlement, 14; the new identity, 74
film strips, 7
fine arts, 41
First Amendment, 76
flash mobs, 35
flipped classroom, 96
Fluent Group, 95
free programs, 11

gamers, 54
Gay and Lesbian Alliance Against Defamation (GLAAD), 73
Gay, Lesbian, and Straight Education Network (GLSEN), 73
gay lifestyles taught in kindergarten, 74
gender: alternate views, 9; confusion, 4, 71; expression, 3; spectrum, 4; traditionalism, 4
gender-based programs, 4
Generation X (Gen X): comparison, 1, 6, 7; and social media, 49
Generation Y (Gen Y): comparison, 8; on steroids, 84
Generation Z (Gen Z): accuracy of work, 85; as colleagues, 19; as entitlement generation, 14; as squishy, 15; at college, 15; bilingual, 62; brains, 95; cause-worthy, 36; cognitive disorders, 18; collaborative networking with, 109; commercial consciousness as consumers, 36, 39; connecting with, 52; decision-making, 51; delicate treatment, 81; digital fluency, 39; digital literacy, 27, 34, 109; digital communication prowess, 106; easily offended, 17, 59; economics of, 85; educational entrepreneurs, 61; ego, 84; ELD, 62; ELL, 62; emotional reasoning, 18, 63; emotions, 96; entertainment, 52; ESL, 62; eye-hand coordination, 38; expectations, 12; fabrications, 82; faster brains, 38, 40; feelings on issues, 89; fickle interests, 86; finances, 86; frustrated by, 89–90; fuzzy future, 54, 55; graduates, 17; highly impulsive, 31; homework effort, 83; ideological inconsistency, 36; impact on American economy, 39; in common with Millennials, 14; inch deep and a mile wide, 21; inordinate expectations, 86; in the marketplace, 84; Internet use, 52; jobs for the future, 65; largest economic impact, 36; learning by videos, 109; lifelong learners, 66; love of devices, 8; loyalty in the marketplace, 20, 36; marketable skills, 110–111; mixing ideologies, 36; multi-switching, 30; multitasking claims, 30, 52, 107; myth of multitasking, 30, 40; narcissism, 106; natural love for learning, 24; neuroscience, 48; non-cognitive skills, 26; outsmarted, 24; parents, 63; political and social justice action, 35; popular applications, 49, 50; post-literate generation, 64; posts feelings online, 28; pragmatism, 36; preparation, 22; prerequisites for college, 84; presidential campaign of 2016, 35; privacy, 50; project-based learning, 54; quick-twitch responses, 38; reaching, 99; recreational mindsets, 57; risk-taking, 60; savvy technology habits, 21, 33, 37; self-esteem, 59; self-perception, 59; shorter attention spans, 38; sleep needs, 37; smart connections, 37; smart enough for life, 32; smarter than technology, 22; social media preferences, 95–96; social uses for devices, 24; stereotype, 88; student-centric, 56; subjective philosophy, 18; successful, 25; teachers of, 41; teaching styles for, 108; technology affinity, 55; Ted Powers on, 60; types of students, 101; unique, 12; want their way, 81–82, 82–83; wheelhouse, 36; wide knowledge, 22; wonderful attributes, 20
George Lucas Educational Foundation, 56
ghetto, 75
Gillett, Rachel, 84
Giuliani, Rudy, 75
global competition, 9
Goleman, Daniel, 31
Google, 54, 60; Classroom, 61; Docs, 61; Play Store, 21; search engine, 64, 91
graduation rates, 9, 12, 22, 34
Great Recession, 84

hands-on skills, 32
Hartman, Joel, 34–35
Harvard University, 65, 84
haters, 72
helicopter parents, 82, 106
Hewlett-Packard, 38
high school, 10
high-tech teacher training institutions, 98
higher education, 16
Holland, Stephen J. F., 18
homework: as thing of the past, 25
homosexual, 73
hyper-gripers, 63
hyphenation nation, 73
hypocrisy, 72

identity: confusion, 5; different, 71; is everything, 70; movement under Obama, 74; politics, 70; protection against offense, 81; self, 5, 6
Illinois, 69
immigrants: non-educated, 2
Immordino-Yang, Helen, 45–46
Instagram, 27, 96
institution-based exam, 23
institutions of higher learning, 16
instructional methods, 11
international competitions, 38
Internet: hacking, 28; parents' use of, 27; propaganda, 12; teachers' use of, 28; use of, 38
interns, 16
iTunes, 21

Jay H. Baker Retailing Center, 84
junior college credit, 32
junior high, 10
Just, Marcel, 48–49

Kahn, Barbara, 84
kind-hearted bureaucrats, 13
kindness of heart, 13
Kini, Tara, 111
Kolb, Lisa, 97

Laliberte, Jean-William, 25
Leahy, Robert L., 18
learning difficulties, 46
Learning Policy Institute, 111

Learn Pop: Teachers Pay Teachers (TpT), 109–110
Lesbian, Gay, Bisexual, Trans, Queer (LGBTQ), 73
liberal voters, 69
linguistic proficiency, 9
literacy rates, 9, 11
literary skills, 65
logic, 52

marriage alternative, 9
Maher, Bill, 17
McGinn, Lata, 18
Mason, Robert, 48–49
massive open online classes (MOOCs), 33, 103
mathematical reasoning, 9
medical advancements, 19
Millennials, 8, 11, 66; as teachers, 1; and social media, 49
money, 7
Moskal, Patsy, 34–35
motivation, 26
multiple choice assessments, 25
music, 95

narcissism, xii, 53
navigation, 32
needs of children, 9
neural connections, 8
neurological issues, 94
neuroscientists, 49
New Jersey, 69
new math, 6
new school, 7
New York, 69
Nintendo, 52
No Child Left Behind (NCLB), 23, 61
North Carolina, 4
Not in My Backyard (NIMBY), 72

Obama, Barack, 23, 74
old school, 7
online bullying and gratification, 29
Oreopoulos, Philip, 25

Pandora, 21
parents: disenchantment, 28; expressions, 28; Gen Z children of, 8; insults from,

Index

28; one-upmanship, 28; social network sites, 29
Pearl Harbor, xi, 8
personal empowerment, 70
Petrilli, Michael, 34
philosophical perspectives, 18
phobic, 72
physical disabilities, 2, 5
physics, 48
Podolsky, Ann, 111
political pressure, 3
politically correct: action, 13, 70; verbiage, 4, 5
political: fairness, 76–77; forces, 20; implications, 19
postsecondary institutions, 16
poverty, 2
power shift, 70
procrastination, 26
Programme for International Student Assessment (PISA), 9
progressive: ideas, 3; legislation, 70
protection from being offended, 17
pseudo-security, 37
psychological puree, 44
public education, 6
purple penguins, 4

Reading across the Curriculum, 6
reality is no longer real, 52
reasonable person test, 17
reprimanded for open debate, 16
reputations ruined, 27
Retana, Alvaro. *See* Hewlett-Packard
Rhode Island Center Prep School, 97
rigors of college entrance, 23
riots, 76
robotics, 32
Rotherham, Andrew, 10

sage on a stage, 108
same-sex marriage, 35, 72
Sanders, Bernie, 36
Schawbel, Dan, 84
Science, Technology, Engineering, Arts, and Mathematics (STEAM), 103
Scholastic Achievement Test (SAT), 23, 24

schools in America: as families, 10, 11; as replacement primary care facilities, 11, 19, 41; as social institutions, 10; safe spaces, 67; secondary, 103–105; supporting families, 11; vast social experiments, 41
secular humanists, 44
Seinfeld, Jerry, 17
self-identity and worship, 5, 6, 70
sensitivities, 16
September 11, 2001, xi, 8
sexual: identity fluidity, 3; photos, 49; preferences, 73
shaming others, 70
shopping on the Internet, 12, 39
Slack, 27, 28, 96
sleep, 8
smart technology: devices, 21, 35, 93; for success, 97; phones, 8; policy, 59
Snapchat, 8, 9, 50, 96, 99
social: divide, 70; empowerment, 70; engineering, 11; inveigling, 9; justice, 13; media posts, 27, 28, 35; networks, 27; programs, 10; status of males and females, 14
Social-Emotional Learning (SEL), 43–44, 45, 65
social media and learning, 112
softest generation, xii, 15
space race, 19
special education, 51
spiritual needs, 44
Stanford University, 54
students: addiction, 58–59; and pathological thinking, 17; and social conditioning, 9; as casualties, 13; as softies, 9, 10; creative thinkers, 49; education centered around, 83; engineered for social causes, 9, 11; impatient, 57; interactions and technology, 94; loan debt, 84; measuring learning, 94; medicated, 2; recording teachers, 27; self-directed learners, 49; smarter than their technology, 21; steeped in social media, 47; subjective philosophy, 18; suggestions to make education better, 90–91; trolling teachers, 28
styles of learning, 11

supplement not supplant, 62
syndromes, 2

takers, 10
Tallahassee, Florida, 13
TD Ameritrade, 85–86
teachers: acting as counselors, 43; adopting policies, 58; appropriate student relationships with, 50, 60; as storytellers, 102; assuming roles of mentors, 56; authenticity, 99; becoming aware of students actions online, 28; being evaluated, 58; being flexible, 54; changing roles, 41; coaching, 43; colleagues, 61; common mission, 112; cutting students slack, 28; effective with Gen Z, 50; fighting back online 28; fine wine and stinky cheese, 111; having goals, 42; in training, 52; leveraging technology, 55; longevity, 112; lounge, 96; making a difference, 107; managing classrooms, 57; passionate about work, 99; persuasive personalities, 100; serving as social case load overseers, 43; technologically literate, 55; time redeemers, 59; using humor, 59–60; using sarcasm, 60; utilizing the Internet, 60; working against progress, 110
teacher preparation, 102–103
teaching as entertainment to reach students, 47, 62
technology: differences, 8; levels of intelligence and utility, 33; modern toy, 49; skills, 26; social and cognitive connections, 36; students' emotions, 31; time stealer, 59
Texas, 3
The Who, 69
Thiel Foundation. *See* Thiel, Peter
Thiel, Peter, 104

thinking styles, 19
thrivers, 25
totalitarianism, 73
touchpad characters, 27
traditional college education, 12, 56
trigger warnings, 17, 60
trophy for everyone, 14
Trump administration, 6
Trump, Donald, 70, 74
trustworthiness 26
truth through feelings, 3, 9
Twitter, 9, 27, 35

unintentional slights, 17
United Kingdom, 103
United States military, 33
University of Pennsylvania (UPenn), 84
University of Pittsburgh, 25
University of Toronto, 25

Values Clarification, 6
VCR, 26
veteran teachers, 19
video games, 8
vindictiveness, 27
viral posts, 28
virtual reality, 103

warning labels on literature, 17
Wharton School of Business. *See* University of Pennsylvania (UPenn)
whole child, 44, 67
WiFi, 98
Wikia, 37
Wilson, Donna, 49
wiring up, 1
word police, 72, 73
World Economic Forum, 65

Yelp, 36
YouTube, 37, 54, 55, 99

About the Author

Ernest J. Zarra III, PhD, currently teaches college preparatory United States government and politics and economics to seniors at the highly state-decorated and top-ranked Centennial High School in Bakersfield, California. Zarra has five earned degrees and holds a PhD from the University of Southern California in teaching and learning theory with cognates in psychology and technology. He is a former Christian College First Team All-American soccer player, former teacher of the year for the prestigious Fruitvale School District, and was awarded the top graduate thesis in education from the California State University at Bakersfield, California.

Zarra has authored six books, including *Helping Parents Understand the Minds and Hearts of Generation Z* (2017), *Common Sense Education: From Common Core to ESSA and Beyond* (2016), *The Wrong Direction for Today's School: The Impact of Common Core on American Education* (2015), and *Teacher-Student Relationships: Crossing into the Emotional, Physical, and Sexual Realms* (2013).

Zarra has written more than a dozen journal articles and professional development programs, is a national conference presenter, former district professional development leader, adjunct university instructor, and a member of several national honor societies. Originally from New Jersey, he and his wife, Suzi, also a teacher, and their two adult children have resided in California for most of their adult lives.

CPSIA information can be obtained
at www.ICGtesting.com
Printed in the USA
BVHW070946071019
560407BV00001B/55/P